She Who Dares Wins

ABOUT THE AUTHORS

Eileen Gillibrand and Jenny Mosley, having both worked successfully for over twenty years in education, counselling, and training in personal development, recognized that there was a need for specialized services for women in these areas. In the eighties, using their combined experiences, expertise and skills, they set up Career Development Counsellors as a company run by women, specifically for women. They now run a comprehensive three stage Career Development Programme which offers individual aptitude and ability testing, a career counselling follow-up interview and a confidence building workshop to support the personal and professional changes women may wish to make in their lives.

Eileen and Jenny have Masters Degrees in Guidance and Counselling, are associate members of the British Association of Counselling and graduate members of the British Psychological Society. They have taught on a wide range of university and technical college courses and are currently involved in university research into how education could do more to counteract the underachievement of young women and to enhance the self-esteem of all young people. Both travel across the UK as consultants to education, industry and the caring services in the areas of promoting self-esteem, developing positive relationships and enhancing management skills. Between them they have written four books and are bringing up six children.

Recognizing that many women are unable to avail themselves of direct personal contact through their career and seminar services, with the support of *New Woman* magazine, they are creating a range of distance learning action packs to encourage women who wish to work on their personal and professional development at home, in their own time.

SHE WHO DARES WINS

**A woman's guide to professional
and personal success**

Eileen Gillibrand & Jenny Mosley

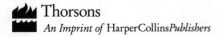
Thorsons
An Imprint of HarperCollins*Publishers*

Thorsons
An Imprint of HarperCollins*Publishers*
77–85 Fulham Palace Road,
Hammersmith, London W6 8JB
1160 Battery Street,
San Francisco, California 94111–1213

Published by Thorsons 1995
1 3 5 7 9 10 8 6 4 2

A catalogue record for this book is available from the British Library

ISBN 0 7225 3036 6

Printed in Great Britain by HarperCollinsManufacturing Glasgow

Contents

FOREWORD

by Anita Roddick, OBE, Founder and Chief Executive of
The Body Shop International plc.

I am constantly asked why there are so few women at the top. I will tell you why: women do not know how exceptional they are and they lack confidence. However, any woman lacking confidence should remember this: if you can figure out which one gets the last toffee, the four year old or the six year old, you can negotiate any contract in the world!

Corporations as we know them have been created by men for men, often influenced by the military model. Hierarchical structures built on authority remain the same. The only way I could challenge this was to set up my own business. But here we are eighteen years later and it is still far easier for any woman to go to a bank and secure a loan for a new kitchen or fitted wardrobe, than it is to get them to agree to lend her money to start a business.

There is a saying: 'where power is, women are not' but for God's sake, please remember the counter-argument to that: if you think you are powerless, you are. Women *must* be willing to be powerful. It is because we bear scars from the ways men have used their power over us that women often want no part of power.

Another of our biggest fears that keeps us from moving ahead with our lives is our difficulty in making decisions ... The irony, of course, is that by not choosing our own path, we *are* choosing which path we follow.

She Who Dares Wins helps women to develop an awareness of their own potential. Via stimulating and interesting exercises, all women can learn something practical to translate into their own lives. Women need to know how other women, from every walk of life, are shaping social, political and economic trends. It is not always possible to devote the time we should to mentoring other women, which I personally believe is a tragedy. *She Who Dares Wins* comes to the rescue by being one of the few self-help books, written *by* women *for* women – 'distance mentoring' on a positive level.

ACKNOWLEDGEMENTS

This book is written by and for women so our first thanks must go to the hundreds of women we have worked with on our various courses over the past twenty years. They gave us invaluable experience, insight and examples with which to write the book. Special thanks must also go to Gill Hudson and Eleni Kyriacou, past and present editors of *New Woman*, for their vision and commitment in encouraging us to create a range of self-development packs for women, and Jane Parmiter, for her originality and tenacity in getting us going in the first place.

We would also like to thank our children, Tom, Cathryn, Ben, David, Meg and Sally for their constant help and interest in our busy lives. Eileen's partner Neville gives consistent encouragement and enthusiasm and Jenny's mother, Veronica Orr, is always a source of inspiration and endless practical support. We have a network of wonderful secretaries and personal assistants all of whom deserve special mention: Neen Dexter, Helen Gowen, Kay Hardwick, Maureen Harvey, Mary Rosser, and Heather Timbrell. Helen Sonnett has been particularly creative in helping to shape some of the ideas.

Our friends, as always, keep us going with their humour and tolerant understanding.

Preface

Traditionally the concept of 'daring' has been mostly associated with men. The qualities of bravery, courage and strength are more likely to be linked with men's actions than with women's. How very limited this way of thinking is. The many everyday pressures on women demand an enormous range of small acts of courage in order to keep going. We would, however, like women to have a greater vision than that of merely 'keeping going'.

Using the resources and qualities they have already developed in order to cope with being women in today's world, it is possible for women to create a stronger vision of what they want and then take that daring leap. 'Daring' leaps are not random, arbitrary, ad hoc gestures. Prior to the 'grand gesture' there must be a series of small, well planned, organized steps.

This book is intended to help women grapple with what they really want from their personal or professional lives. The book demands energy and hard work, both resources that many women already have high quantities of, but very rarely use for their own benefits. We would like women to value their own journeys of personal and professional development as highly as they value helping others to go forward.

In a traditional competitive, male world the image of 'winning' is often associated with a single person bursting through the ranks and leaving others behind. Let's have a different understanding of the word 'winning'. Winning for women would mean working effectively, confidently and quickly within a network of supportive people, sharing their aspirations and hopes.

Any true definition of 'winning' highlights the sense of fulfilment that results from personal efforts. It emphasizes the success that comes from disentangling or liberating oneself. Personal liberation can only come from understanding yourself and knowing what you need to fight for. This book is specifically a self-help book as the act of motivating oneself in order to initiate change and realize potential is the most successful way of ensuring long-term personal benefit and the ability to win.

'Daring' has always been associated with adventure and excitement. Developing your potential is an exciting adventure. It is time that women started to realize that they too can be daring, courageous and adventurous in their efforts to succeed. This self-help book is a first step.

CAN 'SELF-HELP' REALLY WORK?

Research has shown that self-help techniques can profoundly enhance the way you feel about yourself and consequently enable you to adopt a more positive approach to life. When people are feeling depressed, hopeless or miserable it is because they are thinking negative thoughts and feeling pessimistic about the future.

How Does Self-Help Work?

- You have made a decision that you want to change your life. This is the first positive step.
- You are actually making time to tackle your problems. Often people don't set aside proper time to think about their lives.
- It helps you to become self-motivated.
- It shows you how to commit yourself in order to realize your aims.
- It helps you to make realistic decisions about changes you want to make in your life.
- It helps you to take responsibility for your own life and happiness rather than to rely on other people to bring you fulfilment.
- It helps you to develop yourself as a whole person.

This Self-Help Book Will Show You How to

- Enhance your self-image.
- Change negative thought patterns.
- Recognize your self-created myths.
- Believe in your positive qualities.
- Like yourself.
- Recognize and cope with stress.
- Make important changes in your lifestyle.
- Develop positive relationships.
- Take care of your own needs.
- Evaluate your real potential.
- Develop yourself as a whole person.
- Become assertive.
- Maintain a balanced view of your life.
- Make important decisions.
- Make commitments.
- Fulfil personal ambitions.

Completing the questionnaires and worksheets will help you learn the methods and ideas needed to overcome negative thoughts and become a more positive person.

DO WOMEN NEED THIS SELF-HELP BOOK?

... Only if These Statements Ring True to You ...

CIRCLE YOUR RESPONSE

- Women have often been encouraged to put other people's needs first.   ✓ ✗

- Women find it difficult to make regular time to meet their own needs.   ✓ ✗

- Women are judged to be aggressive, pushy or 'unfeminine' if they express their views in the workplace in the same way as men.   ✓ ✗

- Women's contributions at work or home are often more likely to be taken for granted.   ✓ ✗

- Women are likely to have received less attention in mixed schools as a result of teachers responding to the more overt demands of boys.   ✓ ✗

- Women constantly feel guilty at being unable to meet the male media promoted images of the all-successful, all-juggling, all-attractive superwoman.   ✓ ✗

- Women find that, unlike men, their career prospects are less likely to be taken seriously.   ✓ ✗

- Women are worried about seeking out responsibilities or promotion at work as their workplaces often fail to give adequate childcare support.   ✓ ✗

- Women are more likely to have experienced male as opposed to female role models in their personal and professional lives.   ✓ ✗

- Women have to be better qualified than men in order to compete on equal terms.   ✓ ✗

- Women still take on the major share of household and financial management, childcare, and social organization, even if they work.   ✓ ✗

BUT WHY DO WOMEN NEED A SELF-HELP BOOK?

Our past social conditioning has often emphasized the need for women to possess the desirable 'feminine' attributes such as a capacity for caring, nurturing, and passivity. Women are still taught that in order to be considered as good and admirable people they must put others' needs before their own. Despite the growth of feminist philosophy and politics and the continued focus of the women's movement in the media, the fact remains that in many homes, girls are still expected to take on the major share of household tasks whilst observing that expectations are not the same for boys. In schools, too, research continually shows that it is still boys who dominate teachers' time with their more physical and demanding behaviour so that many young women in comprehensive education fail to reach their potential. Statistics inform us that only a few women attain top management positions and, in fact, the figure has dropped over the last ten years from 9.7 per cent to 8.5 per cent. Even in the area of middle management, women only hold 15 per cent of available posts. Why should this be so?

The fairy stories and myths we've been brought up on frequently depict women as helpless creatures waiting to be rescued by 'knights in shining armour' and when interviewed many women still secretly believe that their life will only be fulfilled when the right man enters to rescue them from the drudgery and dross of their everyday existence. This attitude does little to encourage women to seek personal and professional fulfilment in their own right. Moreover, there are too few role models of women in important and demanding careers for other women to aspire to. Girls are far more likely to be surrounded by women supporting others rather than women leading the way.

Those women who do aspire to career prospects are expected to juggle the demands of work with those of the home and of motherhood, leading to the male-controlled media endorsed myth of the 'superwoman'; an impossible role to live up to. Because women are bombarded from all directions with images of the perfect woman, from parents, educators, media and literature, when the reality of their stressful lives fails to match up to the 'ideal' image they have now created for themselves, they then have to cope with the demoralizing burden of guilt. Many women fail to realize their personal and professional potential precisely because they feel guilty about neglecting other people's needs.

Women competing for jobs in a male-dominated workforce, often have to battle against male prejudice for their success, i.e. women are unpredictable, too emotional, subject to hormonal imbalances, not determined enough, unreliable, etc. Also, current managerial models are built on male attributes and men are often unable or unwilling to appreciate that a different approach may be equally successful; they do not want to challenge their own tried and tested approach.

Consider too the Victorian attitudes that have shaped the culture we are brought up in.

Specifically:
A woman's place is in the home.
The way to a man's heart is through his stomach.

Generally:
Spare the rod spoil the child.
Don't blow your own trumpet.
Pride comes before a fall.
Self-praise is no recommendation.
Don't get too big for your boots.
Don't get 'above your station'.

These and other similar little 'gems' have done much to undermine women's self-esteem. This negative Victorian attitude to raising children encouraged many of our parents to place more emphasis on criticism as a means of motivation rather than praise and encouragement. Any form of praise or self-pleasure in success was seen as encouraging 'bigheadedness'; a deadly sin. Consequently many of us were subjected by our teachers or parents to regular 'put downs' in the mistaken belief we would try harder. Many of us continue to regulate our own behaviour through the learnt process of criticism, albeit self-imposed, thereby reinforcing negative self-attitudes. Sadly, praise and encouragement are not experienced as the norm, although most people can look back on childhood experiences and remember how much more willingly and enthusiastically they responded to an adult who gave them praise than any adult who displayed a negative attitude towards them. It is precisely this cultural backdrop that has prevented us from celebrating our strengths and successes with other people and with ourselves.

Do You Personally Need This Book?

	YES	NO
Do you feel frustrated at work or at home?		
Do you feel that you are capable of tackling more?		
Do you look at other more successful people and know that you could do their jobs as well, if not better?		
Do you go to sleep often feeling that you have failed to achieve anything?		
Do you wake up with a low feeling that the day will be boring and unchallenging?		
Do you know that you have more to offer than anyone realizes?		
Do you possess certain skills that you are unable to use in your current lifestyle?		
Do you secretly have career dreams that you fantasize about?		
Do you quietly nurture a desire to learn new work skills?		
Do you secretly wish you could improve your areas of knowledge?		

TAKING RESPONSIBILITY FOR YOUR LIFE

Make a Contract to Help Yourself

1. I understand that I need to make some positive changes in my life.

   Yes ☐

   No ☐

2. I understand that the self-help activities outlined in this book are a necessary part of the process of positive change.

   Yes ☐

   No ☐

3. I will continue to work through this book even though I know that I am going to make excuses, become bored, resentful and fed-up at times.

   Yes ☐

   No ☐

4. I am prepared to put aside ☐ hours a week to spend time meeting my needs as outlined in this book.

5. I understand that my personal and professional development is ultimately my responsibility.

   Yes ☐

   No ☐

   SIGNED:. . . . .

How to Use this Workbook

This workbook is concerned with what you can do to help yourself. It is a self-development programme which you can work through in your own way and at your own pace – in depth over several months, or more superficially over a shorter period of time. It has been designed for you to use on your own or with friends. Working with a friend or colleague is always beneficial and we do suggest that you discuss your ideas and practise the exercises with other people whenever possible.

The book is written for women of all ages, at all stages in their lives, at all levels of ability, living in a partnership or family, with or without children, or living alone.

We have used the term 'partner' throughout to refer to the close permanent relationship in your life, if you have one. We use the word 'work' to cover paid or voluntary work, and 'workplace' to mean your office, factory, shop or home or whatever constitutes a place of work for you. In the same way 'manager' will need to be interpreted to suit your own circumstances.

The approach is based on our fundamental beliefs about woman's development. These are:

- that there is only one person who can take responsibility for your personal development – you.
- that you have the resources within yourself to develop more fully, whatever your circumstances are.
- that you can do it if you really want to.
- that you have to be *fully* committed.
- that a practical step-by-step approach works best.
- that developing your whole self develops your career.
- that she who dares, wins.

Content

The self-development programme focuses on four key issues:

* self-esteem
* stress
* assertiveness
* management skills

The sections are all interrelated and all contribute to the development of your personal and professional potential. Although each section stands alone, maximum benefit will be gained if you work through the book in sequence since many exercises build on strengths and skills developed in earlier sections. You will be guided through a process of self-discovery using questionnaires, information sheets and practical exercises, to explore the issues which are personally holding you back. Step-by-step action plans will show you how to make changes in your life where these are needed.

This is your workbook. Please do write on it, draw on it, highlight it, or do whatever will help you make it your own and aid your learning. As it will probably include personal information, you may want to keep it in a safe place.

What Do You Need to Use this Workbook Successfully?

* *Time.* You do need uninterrupted time to make the most of this opportunity. You will probably need to set aside half an hour at a time, at a minimum, to get properly involved in the reading and exercises. Are there specific times readily available? Can you delegate tasks to others to give you some time? Can you re-organize schedules to make room?

* *A space where you can relax.* Do you have a spare room where you can work? Has your partner/family a weekly commitment when you can claim the sitting room as yours? Can you use your workplace, the library, a friend's house?

* *Courage and support to face change.* Tackling this workbook means that you are prepared to make changes in your thinking and behaviour. Change of any kind is a frightening prospect for many of us, for even though our negative thinking or behaviour may distress or depress us, there is a 'safety' in sticking with them. We know that if we start the painful process of change we may have to face disappointment, disillusion or failure. At least if we are negative we are 'in control'; we are not hoping for positive outcomes or responses from

other people. Part of the self-help process means that you are prepared to seek out support from other people or sources. It is vital that you spend time identifying all the people who you could call on or contact to support you in any personal or professional changes that you may need to make. To start this process fill in the following diagram.

FACING CHANGES WITH SUPPORT

Personal Life

Write in the names of the people who could be supportive if asked.

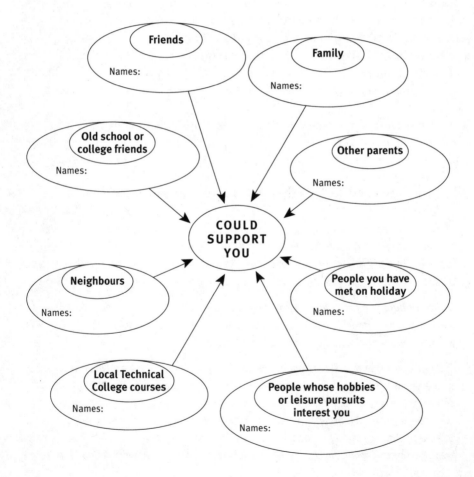

FACING CHANGES WITH SUPPORT

Professional Life

Write in the names of the people who could be supportive if asked.

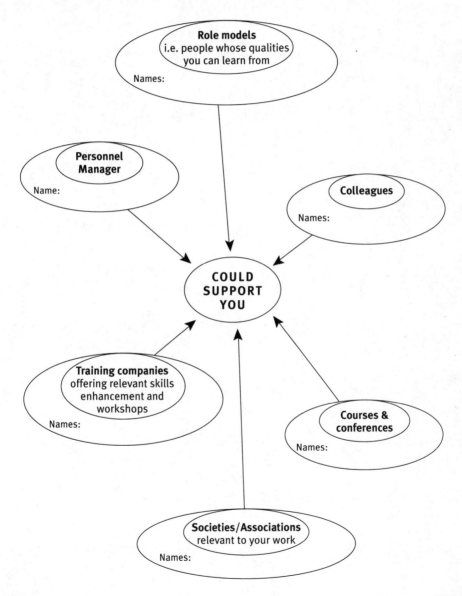

Part one

BUILDING SELF-ESTEEM

We begin with an exploration of self-esteem as it affects every aspect of
your life, the choices that you make, how you relate to others and what you
think you are capable of achieving. You need to learn how to develop a
positive self-image to improve your chances of success in your personal
and professional life.

WHAT IS SELF-ESTEEM?

Self-esteem is the 'inner picture' that we hold of ourselves and our personal strengths and limitations. This self-image affects the way we relate to others, what we think we are capable of achieving and the important choices we make in life.

Look at These Two Questions

Do you value yourself as a worthwhile, likeable and capable person?

or

Do you often suffer from nagging self-doubt, and lack of confidence?

How Will Low Self-Esteem Affect Your Life?

Low self-esteem profoundly affects our lives. It influences how we respond to 'trigger' events or situations in our lives. Low self-esteem can trap us in a downward spiral of failure, in which the negative image we hold of ourselves creates self-fulfilling prophecies. Until we alter this image we will not be free to enjoy any positive progress.

GOOD SELF-ESTEEM ↔ GOOD SELF-CONFIDENCE

GOOD SELF-ESTEEM means: you have a positive self-picture with a strong awareness of your personal strengths and needs. You have a real sense of your own significance and value. You are able to cope with and learn from negative experiences.

leads to

leads to

IMPROVED SELF-CONFIDENCE
Because you are feeling confident, both your verbal and body language 'match up' and convince people of your sincerity. You won't tolerate 'put downs' or unfairness. You challenge people calmly but firmly.

OUTER SELF-CONFIDENCE
You are able to be assertive about your needs, to ask questions, to make choices, decisions and to be tenacious. You have enough confidence to listen well to others and respond to their rights and needs.

leads to

leads to

BETTER SELF-ESTEEM
Because people treat you with respect, listen to you and seek out your opinion, you feel even more valued which enhances your self-image further.

POOR SELF-ESTEEM ↔ POOR SELF-CONFIDENCE

POOR SELF-ESTEEM means: you have a negative self-picture with little awareness of your personal strengths and needs. Low self-worth leads to feelings of insignificance. Negative setbacks or comments tend to overly disappoint or distress you.

leads to

leads to

LOWER SELF-CONFIDENCE
Your relationship skills become poorer. You begin to look passive and flustered. There is a growing mismatch between what you say and your body language, which can betray fear and anxiety.

LOW SELF-CONFIDENCE
You are unable to be clear or direct about expressing your needs or wants. Your fear of failure and lack of confidence mean you fail to challenge authority or ask questions and are easily deterred when things go wrong.

leads to

leads to

LOWER SELF-ESTEEM
You see other people not taking any notice of you or riding roughshod over your feelings which further weakens your self-image and self-evaluation as a person worthy of respect.

5 ■

IS YOUR SELF-ESTEEM GOING UP OR DOWN?

Good Self-Esteem Means ↘

You keep a sense of perspective when life goes wrong.

You are able to develop warm, reciprocal relationships.

You can make positive choices.

You are able to create opportunities for success.

You can admit to mistakes and ask for help.

You make sure your needs are met.

You recognize your skills and aptitudes.

You are prepared to work on your areas of weakness.

You are able to identify your positive qualities.

You can either climb the steps of good self-esteem and greater self-fulfilment or descend the steps of low self-esteem to depression and lack of self-fulfilment.

YOU

You either put yourself down or boost yourself up at the expense of others.

You either deny any areas of weakness or feel a total failure.

You either can't give or accept praise or constantly praise others and still crave approval from others.

You either think everyone is more important than you, or that you are the only person to be considered.

You either become prickly and defensive towards new ideas or slavishly follow every new idea that comes along.

You either can't make decisions and choices or insist that yours are the only ones to follow.

You have troubled or broken relationships.

You either experience frequent failure because you set unrealistic goals or refuse to try anything in case you fail.

You cannot keep hold of a true sense of perspective when life goes wrong.

Low Self-Esteem Means ↗

HOW IS YOUR SELF-ESTEEM?

Private Life

Put a ✓ in the appropriate box

	PART A	NEVER	SOME-TIMES	OFTEN	ALWAYS
1.	Do you see yourself as a likeable and worthwhile person?				
2.	Do you seek out and enjoy new experiences?				
3.	Do you enjoy secure and fulfilling relationships with family and friends?				
4.	Do you have an optimistic approach to life?				
5.	Can you admit to making mistakes?				
6.	Do you consider that you are a capable person?				
7.	Are you happy about meeting new people?				
8.	Do you feel that you are using all your talents and capabilities?				
9.	Do you give yourself time for special treats?				
10.	Do you trust most people?				
11.	Do you experience joy in your life?				
12.	Are you able to relax and have fun?				

Score for Part A:

Never	1
Sometimes	2
Often	3
Always	4

	PART B	NEVER	SOME-TIMES	OFTEN	ALWAYS
13.	Does criticism make you feel totally miserable and/or a failure?				
14.	Are you envious of other women's lives?				
15.	Do you feel other women enjoy more successful relationships than you?				
16.	Do you worry about what people might think of you?				
17.	Do you feel you have to try to 'impress' people with your appearance?				
18.	Do you feel you have to try to 'impress' people with your capabilities?				
19.	Do you feel 'misunderstood' by other people?				
20.	Do you find yourself in situations where you feel excluded?				
21.	Do you find yourself in situations where you feel shy or awkward?				
22.	Do you feel depressed with your life?				
23.	Do you 'miss out' on opportunities to develop areas of your life that you would like to because of outside pressures?				
24.	Do you feel hopeless about your life?				
25.	Do you make excuses for not doing the things you feel you would like to do?				
26.	Do you find yourself, last thing at night, dwelling on all that has gone wrong during the day rather than focusing on something that has gone right?				
27.	Do you try to please other people all the time?				
28.	Do you 'put yourself down' to other people?				
29.	Do you keep problems to yourself?				
30.	Do you secretly dislike people?				

Score for Part B: Never   4
                   Sometimes 3
                   Often   2
                   Always   1

Results

Score 30–45   Your self-esteem is generally low so you need to find ways to enhance it in order to enjoy a more fulfilling personal life. Perhaps it is time to realize that you *can* feel good about yourself and learn how to initiate changes in your private life, which will enhance your self-image, your relationships and, in time, make you feel happier in yourself.

Score 46–75   Your self-esteem is fluctuating and still needs to be enhanced. You need to feel more confident in your ability to cope and more able to put yourself forward. Perhaps earlier experiences have left you vulnerable in certain areas; this now needs to be recognized and dealt with.

Score 76–104   In general you have quite sound self-esteem, but certain specific areas are still causing you problems and need to be dealt with if you are to feel fully confident about yourself and able to really make the most out of opportunities that come your way.

Score 105–120   You enjoy a high level of self-esteem and are confident in your outlook on life. Perhaps it is now time to set yourself fresh challenges and consider exciting and new initiatives in your quest for personal fulfilment.

Professional Life

Put a ✓ in the appropriate box

	PART A	NEVER	SOME-TIMES	OFTEN	ALWAYS
1.	Are you happy with your work?				
2.	Do you feel appreciated at work?				
3.	Does your job suit your capabilities?				
4.	Do you get on well with colleagues?				
5.	Do you enjoy a good relationship with your boss?				
6.	Are you able to meet work deadlines?				
7.	Are you happy to learn new skills?				
8.	Would you welcome promotion and additional responsibilities?				
9.	Do you feel confident and relaxed at work?				
10.	Can you delegate work confidently to other people?				
11.	Is your work fulfilling and rewarding?				
12.	Do you feel successful at work?				
13.	Do you fit in at work?				
14.	Do you consider your views are important at work?				
15.	Do you feel confident in dealing with work situations?				
16.	Do you feel you are progressing at a satisfactory rate?				
17.	Do you have achievable goals that you are aiming for?				
18.	Do you think you are reliable and conscientious?				

Score for Part A: Never   1
Sometimes 2
Often   3
Always   4

	PART B	NEVER	SOME-TIMES	OFTEN	ALWAYS
19.	Do you find disagreements which arise between colleagues and yourself difficult to resolve?				
20.	Do you feel that your work does little to enhance your image to other people?				
21.	Do you feel your manager or colleagues treat you with a lack of respect?				
22.	Do you have difficulty initiating new ideas or schemes at work?				
23.	Are you alarmed by new tasks?				
24.	Do you worry about the standard of your work?				
25.	Are you anxious about making a mistake in your work?				
26.	Are you envious of other people's roles at work?				
27.	Do you feel other people at work are more favoured than you are?				
28.	Do you worry about work after you have left the workplace?				
29.	Do you complain about situations/events at work?				
30.	Do you think other people have more exciting/interesting jobs?				

Score for Part B: Never   4
                     Sometimes   3
                     Often   2
                     Always   1

Results

Score 30–45   Your self-esteem in your workplace is generally low and changes evidently need to be made. Perhaps you are in the wrong job and need to consider a complete change; otherwise you need to sort out the areas where improvements can be made and decide on a plan of action to implement them.

Score 46–75   There are still work areas that need improving in order for you to be fully satisfied with your professional life. Try and isolate the areas of concern that need to be dealt with so that you can be more effective in achieving job satisfaction and success. You still have an unclear self-picture of all your qualities and are unable to make the most of any opportunities that arise.

Score 76–104   Your self-esteem at work is generally sound so you can concentrate on those areas where you achieved a low score and find ways to make the necessary improvements. Perhaps it is time to set some fresh challenges or learn a new skill and boost your confidence even further.

Score 105–120 Your self-esteem is high and you seem to be brimming with confidence, but have you set yourself sufficiently high goals? Perhaps now is the time to consider a new challenge or seek exciting fresh horizons.

UNDERSTANDING YOUR NEEDS

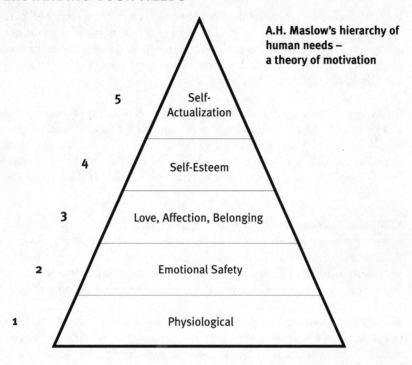

**A.H. Maslow's hierarchy of human needs –
a theory of motivation**

5   Self-Actualization

4   Self-Esteem

3   Love, Affection, Belonging

2   Emotional Safety

1   Physiological

One of the most significant theories of motivation is A.H. Maslow's hierarchy of human needs. Maslow proposed that individuals need to satisfy the following needs. If these needs are consequently unmet, our inner personal and professional potential is unable to surface through the 'layers' of stress and frustration.

1. **Physiological needs**. These are the most basic needs and include our need for food and rest and to be physically fit. We already know that many women have an uneasy relationship with food which results in various illnesses. Equally, demands of careers and children can often mean that women are constantly exhausted and unable to give time to becoming physically healthy.

2. **Safety needs**. These needs involve living in a safe and secure physical and emotional environment. All people need to feel 'safe' in their lives; if they are constantly emotionally or physically vulnerable they cannot take important risks. Women often place themselves in unsafe physical and emotional situations which then keep them from being able to face the risks and uncertainties of making positive changes in their lives.

3. **Need for love, affection and belonging**. These needs involve our desire to be accepted and liked. Reference to this level shows us why it is particularly important for women to network with other women and to give and receive support from women. Because of the breakdown in safety of the extended family in addition to severe financial pressure, many women do now find themselves in isolated positions.

4. **Self-esteem**. We all need to receive recognition, appreciation and attention for our contributions. If we are being taken for granted, ignored or 'put down' we will be unable to sustain a positive self-image and begin to undervalue or negate our achievements.

5. **Self-actualization**. Maslow stated that once all these basic needs are met, we move onto needing to realize our inner potential, in other words, we all need the chance to access our natural creativity; i.e. the opportunity to experiment with ideas, to succeed at certain tasks, to make autonomous decisions.

ARE YOUR UNMET NEEDS HOLDING YOU BACK?

Draw a circle around any of the areas listed below which are currently affecting you. Perhaps you have become 'stuck' at one level because your needs here are not being met and this is preventing you from moving onto a higher level of fulfilment, thereby realizing your true personal and professional potential.

5. SELF-ACTUALIZATION OR SELF POTENTIAL

Few opportunities to make decisions	Lack of time or opportunity to be creative	Few chances to effect changes in personal or professional life	No opportunity to contribute to a positive vision of the future

4. SELF-ESTEEM

Constant criticism Rare praise	No chance to use range of skills that you are capable of	Few opportunities to 'shine' at work or home	Few opportunities to have success

3. AFFECTION AND BELONGING

Isolated/Lonely	Unwelcoming workplace	Lack of love/affection in your relationships	Unreliable friends

2. SAFETY

Insecure relationships	Job insecurity	Physical threats/abuse. Bullying at work or home	Backbiting from 'friends' or colleagues

1. PHYSIOLOGICAL

Unhealthy eating	Lack of home security, insufficient rest	Poor health/ dependence on alcohol, cigarettes, pills	Lack of physical fitness

UNDERSTANDING YOUR SELF-ESTEEM

During our lives we all encounter negative statements from influential people that have affected the way we see ourselves. Some of the following comments may sound familiar.

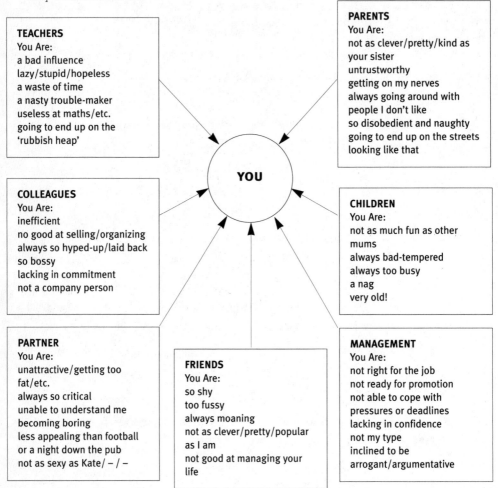

PARENTS
You Are:
not as clever/pretty/kind as your sister
untrustworthy
getting on my nerves
always going around with people I don't like
so disobedient and naughty
going to end up on the streets
looking like that

TEACHERS
You Are:
a bad influence
lazy/stupid/hopeless
a waste of time
a nasty trouble-maker
useless at maths/etc.
going to end up on the 'rubbish heap'

COLLEAGUES
You Are:
inefficient
no good at selling/organizing
always so hyped-up/laid back
so bossy
lacking in commitment
not a company person

YOU

CHILDREN
You Are:
not as much fun as other mums
always bad-tempered
always too busy
a nag
very old!

PARTNER
You Are:
unattractive/getting too fat/etc.
always so critical
unable to understand me
becoming boring
less appealing than football or a night down the pub
not as sexy as Kate/ – / –

FRIENDS
You Are:
so shy
too fussy
always moaning
not as clever/pretty/popular as I am
not good at managing your life

MANAGEMENT
You Are:
not right for the job
not ready for promotion
not able to cope with pressures or deadlines
lacking in confidence
not my type
inclined to be arrogant/argumentative

Statements such as these may well have negatively affected your self-esteem. It is important to understand this so that you can distance yourself from the past in order to make positive choices and changes in the future. You don't have to continue to reflect other peoples' prejudices, preferences or negativity. You are capable of creating your own self-image.

UNDERSTANDING YOUR SELF-ESTEEM

Now identify negative comments from your past that you think have directly affected the way you see yourself.

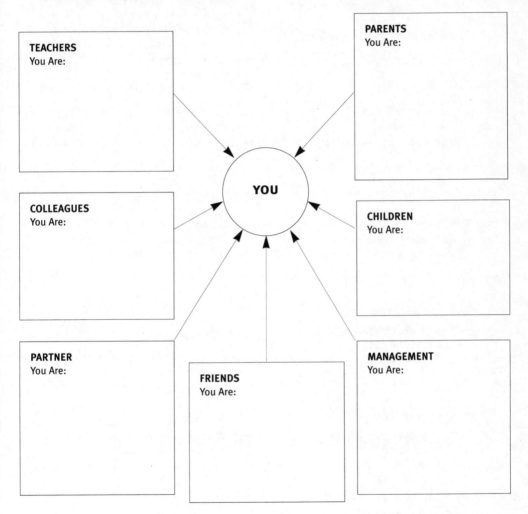

Select those statements which you feel are untrue or come from that person's own negative attitudes. Write these statements down on a piece of paper and then tear it up. As you do this, make a conscious decision to eliminate these negative images from how you see yourself.

THE DOWNWARD SPIRAL OF LOW SELF-ESTEEM

1. **NEGATIVE SELF-BELIEF**
Negative comments from others, past failures and negative experiences become internalized into feelings of low self-worth.

You take on board all the criticisms and negative experiences and believe them to be true or your fault. Self-esteem is eroded and you start to lose confidence in yourself as a worthwhile person.

2. **POOR SELF-IMAGE**
Lack of confidence is conveyed to others

Your lack of confidence and negative self-image is seen by others as the 'real' you.

3. **LOW EXPECTATIONS**
Little is expected by both yourself and others.

You are not seen by yourself or others as someone who is very capable or innovative.

4. **FEWER OPPORTUNITIES**
You don't create opportunities for success and others don't give them to you.

You don't risk any new challenges and others don't have any faith in you so they don't offer any either.

5. **POOR PERFORMANCE**
Little opportunity to develop and to practise skills.

Your skills and aptitudes diminish further as you have little opportunity to enhance or develop them.

REINFORCED NEGATIVE SELF-BELIEF
Your original feelings of low self-worth become a self-fulfilling prophecy and you feel diminished as a person.

THE UPWARD SPIRAL OF SOUND SELF-ESTEEM

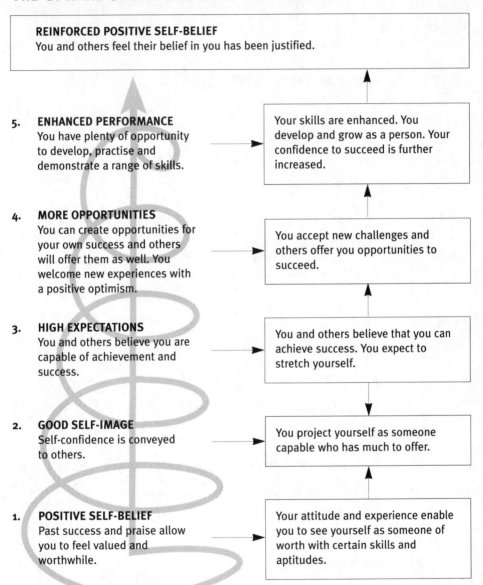

REINFORCED POSITIVE SELF-BELIEF
You and others feel their belief in you has been justified.

5. **ENHANCED PERFORMANCE**
You have plenty of opportunity to develop, practise and demonstrate a range of skills.

Your skills are enhanced. You develop and grow as a person. Your confidence to succeed is further increased.

4. **MORE OPPORTUNITIES**
You can create opportunities for your own success and others will offer them as well. You welcome new experiences with a positive optimism.

You accept new challenges and others offer you opportunities to succeed.

3. **HIGH EXPECTATIONS**
You and others believe you are capable of achievement and success.

You and others believe that you can achieve success. You expect to stretch yourself.

2. **GOOD SELF-IMAGE**
Self-confidence is conveyed to others.

You project yourself as someone capable who has much to offer.

1. **POSITIVE SELF-BELIEF**
Past success and praise allow you to feel valued and worthwhile.

Your attitude and experience enable you to see yourself as someone of worth with certain skills and aptitudes.

THE DOWNWARD SPIRAL OF LOW SELF-ESTEEM

Personal Life

Example

1. **NEGATIVE SELF-BELIEF**
   I'm no good with people.

2. **POOR SELF-IMAGE**
   Self: I'm boring, I wish I could talk to people more easily.
   Others think: She seems a bit dull and stand-offish.

3. **LOW EXPECTATIONS**
   Self: I'll never change.
   Others think: She doesn't seem to want to make friends – she seems to like her own company.

4. **FEWER OPPORTUNITIES**
   Self: I don't think I'll go to that party. I'll only stand in a corner and feel miserable.
   Others think: She won't come, she doesn't seem to like mixing, I won't bother asking her again.

5. **POOR PERFORMANCE**
   Self: I'm becoming more shy and nervous.
   Others think: She shows no interest in other people. She's very cold and rude.

REINFORCED NEGATIVE SELF-BELIEF
I knew I was no good with people. I shouldn't even try to socialize, it's a waste of time.

THE UPWARD SPIRAL OF SOUND SELF-ESTEEM

Personal Life

Example

REINFORCED POSITIVE SELF-BELIEF
It's really great to have a good social life and meet so many interesting people.

---

5. ENHANCED PERFORMANCE
Self: Everyone is so different. No-one frightens me anymore. It's really enjoyable drawing people out and learning about their different lives.
Others think: She's always an asset to any gathering.

4. MORE OPPORTUNITIES
Self: It's good to have so many different chances to go out.
Others think: We must invite her, she's such a good laugh and always makes us feel as if we have got a lot to offer.

3. HIGH EXPECTATIONS
Self: I'll have a good social life and meet plenty of people.
Others think: She always puts people at ease and helps to get a party going.

2. GOOD SELF-IMAGE
Self: I like making friends and having interesting conversations.
Others think: She's a warm, friendly person.

1. POSITIVE SELF-BELIEF
I enjoy meeting new people.

THE DOWNWARD SPIRAL OF LOW SELF-ESTEEM

Professional Life

Example

1. **NEGATIVE SELF-BELIEF**
   I'm not good enough for promotion.

2. **POOR SELF-IMAGE**
   Self: I haven't got what it takes to get on.
   Others think: She doesn't seem to have much
   ambition or confidence in herself.

3. **LOW EXPECTATIONS**
   Self: It's probably best to stay within this
   department.
   Others think: She seems quite happy to stay
   put in her present position.

4. **FEWER OPPORTUNITIES**
   Self: I don't think I'll apply for this promotion.
   Others think: No good asking her to apply, she
   doesn't have the commitment or interest.

5. **POOR PERFORMANCE**
   Self: My work is suffering because I'm bored
   and discouraged.
   Others think: She'll never better herself. She is
   becoming careless and slipshod.

REINFORCED NEGATIVE SELF-BELIEF
I'll never get on and reach a higher level.

THE UPWARD SPIRAL OF SOUND SELF ESTEEM

Professional Life

Example

REINFORCED POSITIVE SELF-BELIEF
I knew I could get on if I tried.

5. **ENHANCED PERFORMANCE**
   Self: I'm doing well and I have learnt so much.
   Others think: She's made very good progress.

4. **MORE OPPORTUNITIES**
   Self: I'll go to this seminar and learn that new skill.
   Others think: She is a good 'bet' to send on the course.

3. **HIGH EXPECTATIONS**
   Self: I might even reach the board of directors one day.
   Others think: She should go far, she has the right attitude.

2. **GOOD SELF-IMAGE**
   Self: I think I could get promotion if I tried.
   Others think: She seems a 'go ahead' type.

1. **POSITIVE SELF-BELIEF**
   I could get on in this job.

POSITIVE THINKING CAN CHANGE YOUR LIFE

You will have seen from the previous spiral diagrams how a self-belief can influence and affect your lifestyle for better or for worse.

Self-beliefs not only affect how you choose to live your life and what you believe yourself capable of doing, but they also influence how other people perceive you and what their attitudes towards you will be.

If the self-belief is negative, it will limit your personal and professional development. You will avoid situations which 'test' this belief and other people will see it as an area in which you have little potential.

If, however, the self-belief is positive, you will have greater opportunity to develop and grow as a person. Other people will have faith in your capability and offer you even more experiences in which you can enhance your skills and learn new ones. Your confidence will be increased, leading you on further to 'bigger and better' things.

It is, therefore, important to take the negative self-beliefs you have and turn them into more positive statements about yourself, so that you can change the downward spiral of low self-esteem into an upward spiral of sound self-esteem and thereby enjoy the benefits that this will bring to you.

THE DOWNWARD SPIRAL OF LOW SELF-ESTEEM

Personal Life

Choose a negative self-belief from your personal life that you think is true about yourself. Use the previous examples to help you write down the sort of statements you might make about yourself and what other people might think.

Examples

1. **NEGATIVE SELF-BELIEF**

2. **POOR SELF-IMAGE**
   Self:

   Others think:

3. **LOW EXPECTATIONS**
   Self:

   Others think:

4. **FEWER OPPORTUNITIES**
   Self:

   Others think:

5. **POOR PERFORMANCE**
   Self:

   Others think:

REINFORCED NEGATIVE SELF-BELIEF

THE UPWARD SPIRAL OF SOUND SELF-ESTEEM

Personal Life

Now take the previous negative statement, but make it more positive and, using the previous examples given to help you, fill in the diagram below.

Examples

REINFORCED POSITIVE SELF-BELIEF

5. **ENHANCED PERFORMANCE**
Self:

Others think:

4. **MORE OPPORTUNITIES**
Self:

Others think:

3. **HIGH EXPECTATIONS**
Self:

Others think:

2. **GOOD SELF-IMAGE**
Self:

Others think:

1. **POSITIVE SELF-BELIEF**

THE DOWNWARD SPIRAL OF LOW SELF-ESTEEM

Professional Life

Now repeat this process for a negative self-belief from your professional life.

Examples

1. **NEGATIVE SELF-BELIEF**

2. **POOR SELF-IMAGE**
   Self:

   Others think:

3. **LOW EXPECTATIONS**
   Self:

   Others think:

4. **FEWER OPPORTUNITIES**
   Self:

   Others think:

5. **POOR PERFORMANCE**
   Self:

   Others think:

REINFORCED NEGATIVE SELF-BELIEF

THE UPWARD SPIRAL OF SOUND SELF-ESTEEM

Professional Life

Now make this self-belief into a more positive statement and fill in the diagram.

Examples

REINFORCED POSITIVE SELF-BELIEF

5. **ENHANCED PERFORMANCE**
   Self:

   Others think:

4. **MORE OPPORTUNITIES**
   Self:

   Others think:

3. **HIGH EXPECTATIONS**
   Self:

   Others think:

2. **GOOD SELF-IMAGE**
   Self:

   Others think:

1. **POSITIVE SELF-BELIEF**

CHALLENGING NEGATIVE THINKING

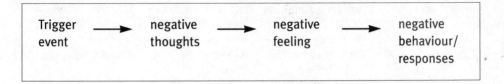

Trigger event ⟶ negative thoughts ⟶ negative feeling ⟶ negative behaviour/ responses

Everyone experiences negative thoughts and feelings, ranging from mild irritation and frustration through to troughs of deep depression, anger or unhappiness. Negative thoughts affect the way you feel and this, in turn, influences the way in which you behave. It is possible, however, to change how you think and feel and so exert more control over your life. You do not have to be a helpless victim of circumstances; you can learn to change negative thought patterns through positive responses and enjoy a far greater freedom of choice in your life.

Negative thoughts arise when something goes wrong or something 'bad' happens to us; for example, you lose your job, you suffer an illness, a trusted friend talks behind your back, someone you care for moves away, or you are unfairly criticized. It is perfectly natural to experience sadness, frustration or anger when a difficult event occurs, but sometimes this can continue and become a repeated pattern leading to loss of self-esteem and depression. Moods are determined by what you think and how you view any given situation. Research shows that with determination and practice you can change your perception of a situation from a negative to a positive one.

You will find that certain 'trigger' events in your life produce familiar patterns of negative thought.

Example

TRIGGER EVENT	NEGATIVE THOUGHTS	NEGATIVE FEELINGS	NEGATIVE BEHAVIOUR
Loss of job	Bad things always happen to me. They got rid of me because I am no good.	anger, resentment, feeling of worthlessness	Fail to apply for other jobs
Ending of a relationship	I'm so alone. I'll never get over this loss. I'll never feel happy again. No one will ever care for me again.	sadness, loneliness, self-pity	Don't go out anymore
Unkind personal comment from a friend	People don't really like me. I haven't anything to offer other people.	sadness, resentment, loss of self-esteem	Fail to initiate or contribute to friendship
Losing your temper	I'm so out of control. Why was I so cruel to someone I cared about. I really hate myself.	remorse, guilt, anger at self	Bottle up things
Making a mistake	What will the consequences be? How could I behave so stupidly? I wish I was dead?	guilt, fear, embarrassment	Refuse to tackle new situations
Illness	What's going to happen? What if I'm never well again? Why did this happen to me? I don't deserve this.	Pessimistic, discouraged, depressed	Move toward a full depression

Think of four trigger events, two from your personal life and two from your professional life, that have produced negative feelings and thoughts in your life and write them into the columns below.

TRIGGER EVENT	NEGATIVE THOUGHTS	NEGATIVE FEELINGS	NEGATIVE BEHAVIOUR
1. Personal Life			
2. Personal Life			
3. Professional Life			
4. Professional Life			

You are now going to explore ten ways to combat negative thinking which you can use to help you overcome the stressful feelings and moods you are experiencing.

It is important that you realize that only you have the power to effect changes in the way that you think and these changes can have a dramatic impact on your life, and empower you to enjoy greater fulfilment and happiness.

TEN WAYS TO CHALLENGE NEGATIVE THINKING

1. BE REALISTIC	Write down your negative thought. Is it really logical or has it become distorted or over exaggerated? Are you blaming yourself or others entirely for this problem? Sort out parts of your thought which are not necessarily true.	Rewrite your thought, discarding the illogical, emotional or distorted parts and substitute them with more positive statements.
EXAMPLE	*I've lost my job. I'm a born loser.*	*I am temporarily unemployed but hope to find work soon.*

2. SEARCH FOR THE TRUTH	Some negative thoughts are simply not true; they arise out of your own bad feelings about yourself.	Recognize the lie in this type of thought and re-think a positive and more truthful statement.
EXAMPLE	*My extrovert colleague doesn't like me, because I'm not her type.*	*People can appreciate each other's differences with some insight, understanding and tolerance. Maybe I could be less reserved with her.*

3. EXAMINE THE PROS AND CONS	Write down your negative thought and then in two separate columns list the pros and cons of thinking this way. Be as searching and truthful as you can in this exercise. Tot up the statements in each column to see which has the most.	Evaluate how much benefit/harm this thought is having on your life. Resolve to discard or amend the thought if it will bring you greater benefit.
EXAMPLE	*John has forgotten to give me a birthday card and I'm really angry with him.*	*This negative thought and the bad feeling it creates is causing more harm than good. I could deal with it and then discard it through discussion with honesty and warmth.*

John has forgotten to give me a birthday card and I'm really angry with him.

Pros	Cons
I feel justified in sulking. I want to punish John for hurting me then I'll feel the pain is balanced.	*My feeling of resentment is hurting me as well. I'm losing John's company as he's avoiding my bad mood. We're moving apart. We're both erecting barriers against future pain.*

TOTAL	2	4

4. BE KIND TO YOURSELF	Many people punish and belittle themselves for mistakes far more than they would another person. You might find it harder to forgive yourself than you would someone else.	Be as kind and forgiving to yourself as you would to someone else. Offer yourself the same kind of positive suggestions you would offer to a friend.
EXAMPLE	*I forgot to ask my sister how her exam went and she was upset with me. How could I be so thoughtless and inconsiderate as to forget something this important? I'm a really uncaring and selfish person. I don't deserve her love.*	*Oh no! Fancy forgetting something as important as this. Perhaps I could buy her a nice card and some flowers to show her how sorry I am and how much I really care about her. Still everybody forgets things sometimes, I'm only human.*

5. FACE UP TO YOUR FEARS	Write down your negative thought and then decide exactly why it bothers you so much. You will probably find there are underlying fears and anxieties which you could deal with.	Resolve to work on any fears and anxieties in a positive way so that you can alleviate the negative responses they evoke.
EXAMPLE	*I hate going to parties and often I invent a headache or another excuse to avoid them. Why? I am nervous of meeting strangers. I don't have any small talk and they'll think I'm really stupid or boring.*	*I could develop a hobby or read books to gain more information and general 'chat'. I could practise opening conversations and rehearse what I am going to say in my mind. I could even get a friend to help me improve my conversational skills.*

6. BANISH GENERALIZATIONS	Write down your negative thought then ask yourself if you are making any sweeping generalizations which are inaccurate and preventing logical thought.	Understand that specific negative behaviour does not necessarily apply 'across the board' and can be seen in its true perspective.
EXAMPLE	*One of the senior partners was snappy with me at work when I asked for advice, so I'm never going to approach him again. I don't like him because he's so unpredictable.*	*Realistically, he was always pleasant enough before that occasion. Perhaps he was under pressure or not feeling well and I should really not allow one bad incident to determine my future feelings towards him.*

7. FOCUS ON ALL THE FACTORS	Write down your negative thought and examine it to see if you have taken all the factors into consideration. Are you putting too much emphasis on your own or other people's behaviour without knowing the full circumstances?	By acknowledging that other factors are involved you lessen the emphasis you had previously placed on youself or others. This can then decrease the degree of negativity you are feeling.
EXAMPLE	*I didn't get promotion. I feel really depressed about it and worthless. I don't think I'll apply again because I won't be considered.*	*Actually, the other person got the job because she had certain skills and experience that were considered more appropriate in this instance. That doesn't detract from my capabilities and I should not allow this failure to deter my career ambitions.*

8. ASSUMPTIONS CAN BE FALSE	Some negative thoughts are based on false assumptions. You may be attributing other people's behaviour to the wrong motives.	Check out that what you believe to be true is actually so.
EXAMPLE	*David won't take me to the pub because he's embarrassed to be seen out with me.*	*I now know that David doesn't take me to the pub out of consideration for my feelings. His mates are bawdy and loud and he thinks I would feel uncomfortable with them and not enjoy myself. He's happy to go on a different night with me.*

9. CHECK THE VALIDITY OF YOUR FEELINGS	You may have negative feelings about certain things and feel depressed because you have them, but in some areas negative feelings are quite usual and you will not be alone in your fears.	Talk to other people about these negative feelings to see if they have experienced them as well. Perhaps they are a normal reaction to a given situation and not something to become depressed about.
EXAMPLE	*My youngest child has just started school. I feel miserable, depressed and lonely without her. There must be something wrong with me to feel like this.*	*I have talked to other mothers and some of them felt exactly as I do. They have been very helpful in suggesting ways I can deal with these negative feelings.*

10. ACCEPT YOUR NEGATIVE THOUGHTS	In this method, influenced by eastern thinking, you accept your negative feelings with tranquillity instead of fighting against them.	Accept that these negative thoughts are part of your make-up as a human being and that they are not a reason for becoming depressed.
EXAMPLE	*I'm not a very reliable person. I break appointments, arrive late and sometimes let people down. I hate myself for this and feel really bad about not living up to other people's expectations.*	*I accept that as a human being I have certain shortcomings. Many people still like me in spite of these and I cannot realistically expect to be perfect.*

CHALLENGE YOUR OWN NEGATIVE THOUGHTS

Choose two recent negative thoughts you have experienced in your personal and professional life and now write them down in the middle columns. Re-read 'Ten Ways to Challenge Negative Thinking' and select an appropriate method and write in the first box. Now take the time to write in the last box the new positive change you have made in your thinking.

Personal Life

METHOD USED	NEGATIVE THOUGHT	POSITIVE CHANGE

Professional Life

METHOD USED	NEGATIVE THOUGHT	POSITIVE CHANGE

LOOKING FOR THE POSITIVE IN YOUR SITUATION

Many women have become so accustomed to negative thinking about themselves that they are unable to look for the positive advantage in their situations. Positive thinking always helps to change your perspective about things so make a list of your 'moans' and then try to find one positive statement to make about each one.

Examples in Personal Life

MOAN	POSITIVE ADVANTAGE
I'm stuck at home with the kids all day.	I'm passing on lots of my talents and personal qualities to the kids.
My social life is so hectic I feel completely frazzled.	People seem to seek out my company; they must find me interesting and worthwhile.

Now fill in two of your own examples

MOAN	POSITIVE ADVANTAGE

LOOKING FOR THE POSITIVE IN YOUR SITUATION

Examples in Professional Life

Make another list of 'moans' for your professional life and try to find one positive statement to make about each one.

MOAN	POSITIVE ADVANTAGE
I've got too many deadlines to meet.	Deadlines are really helping me get through a range of tasks very quickly.
Our office is so noisy and busy it's hard to concentrate.	It's good to have people around to chat to sometimes and there's always something interesting going on.

Now fill in two of your own examples

MOAN	POSITIVE ADVANTAGE

EMPOWERING YOURSELF

Questions that help us to release energy and fulfil our potential – put a ✓ or ✗ beside each

FULFILLING YOUR SPIRITUAL SELF
Do I know how to practise inner relaxation strategies?
Do I ever explore other religions, yoga or meditation?
Do I take time to observe areas of natural beauty and power?

EMOTIONAL NEEDS
Do I need to make new friends?
Can I develop a stable relationship with a partner if I want to?
Can I express my feelings?
Can I cry, shout, laugh in my own home?
Do I have times when people can show their love to me?

FULFILLING YOUR COGNITIVE SELF
Do I get time to think things through, structure ideas and plans?
Do I read books, see stimulating films or plays?
Do people ask me for my ideas and value my contributions?
Do I spend time debating and reflecting?

EMPOWERING YOURSELF

FULFILLING YOUR CREATIVE SELF
Do I ever make opportunities to look at beautiful paintings?
Do I get the chance to play with textured materials, to write poems, to listen or move to music?
Do I get the opportunity to develop creative hobbies?
Do I ever sing freely?

FULFILLING YOUR PHYSICAL SELF
Do I feel physically safe from harm?
Do I feel fit?
Do I get adequate sleep?
Do I have regular exercise?
Do I have a healthy well balanced diet?
Do I explore and feel comfortable with my sexuality?

These are areas that will help us to develop ourselves fully. We, personally, can take responsibility for our decision to pursue or not to pursue these areas of our self-potential.

GIVE YOURSELF GOOD ADVICE

When you become upset or depressed, it is your feelings that have gone awry; it's not that you have become a useless person. Compassionate, sound advice is helpful in making your thoughts more objective and less negative, but most people give themselves a hard time for the way they feel and for their supposed shortcomings; yet this is simply an illogical response.

Imagine that a close friend has recently broken up with her partner. She is depressed and feels rejected and unlovable. Would you tell her, 'Of course he dumped you, it's all your fault, you're no good. How could you possibly expect anyone would find you attractive or love you!'? Of course you wouldn't. You would try to soothe her pain and raise her self-esteem by comforting and encouraging her with positive statements about herself. You would let her know that she is a worthwhile person with many great qualities. You would realize that this person needed boosting up, so that she could feel valued again. You would not bombard her with a list of negative points about herself which would only reinforce her low self-esteem.
If you can see the logic in treating a friend like this, then you must surely realize that you need to talk to yourself in the same manner, if you want to regain good feelings about yourself. There are two active practical exercises that are very helpful in doing this.

I am my Friend

Ask a friend, partner or family member to help you in this, making sure that it is someone you feel comfortable with and trust. The other person will play your negative self and will read out to you a list of all the bad things you think about yourself, which you have previously written down. This negative list should be said in the first person, as though she were talking about herself.

You will adopt the role of your positive self and argue against all the negative points, putting them into true perspective. Also, emphasize her (your) positive qualities. If you find this hard to do and are feeling so depressed that you cannot think of anything good to say about yourself, ask the friend to swap roles so that she can make the positive statements.

Mirror, Mirror on the Wall

Look into a mirror and tell your reflection all the bad things that you think about yourself. Now, continue to look at your reflection, but imagine that it is a dear friend. Give this friend good, sound and helpful advice. Set out to boost her self-esteem and make her feel better about herself. Be as positive and caring as if you were actually talking to a friend and not yourself. Look at your reflection as though you really liked this 'person' and were considerate of her feelings.

I am my Friend

Example personal life

NEGATIVE SELF	POSITIVE SELF
I'm unattractive and I don't think people really like me.	You have lovely eyes and hair. How about trying a new image – change your style of clothes. You do have real friends who care about you because you are funny and generous and always caring.
I'm putting on weight.	What about joining a slimming club or taking up a regular sporting commitment.
I don't seem to be good at anything.	You're very good at cooking, remembering birthdays, organizing other people, interior decor.
I always feel fed up and miserable.	Why don't you think of something that makes you feel really good and plan to do it. Think of things that would help you feel better and work towards achieving them. Perhaps join a self-help group to encourage you.

I am my Friend

Find someone to try out this technique with. Afterwards record the main points of your conversation on the diagram below, so that you can look back and remember how helpful it was to you.

NEGATIVE SELF	POSITIVE SELF

I am my Friend

Example professional life

NEGATIVE SELF	POSITIVE SELF
I'm not getting anywhere at work.	You didn't always feel like this; why have you lost interest? Perhaps you should re-evaluate what you want in a job.
I'm so inefficient and uninterested.	Maybe it's time to change direction or move on. You used to be very enthusiastic, so you could be again if you find the right motivating factor.
I don't want to go in the mornings and I'm always the first to leave at night.	
I never volunteer for anything or opt to join in any seminars.	Set yourself one small achievable work-target each week. You contributed good ideas in the past; with pre-planning you could do this again.
I just don't care about it anymore.	Everyone has stale patches at work; it might pass. Try livening up your social life. Think seriously of a new challenge. Have a chat with your boss or take a holiday and see if you feel better after a break.

I am my Friend

Find someone to try out this technique with. Afterwards record the main points of your conversation on the diagram below, so that you can look back and remember how helpful it was to you.

NEGATIVE SELF	POSITIVE SELF

Mirror, Mirror on the Wall

Personal Life
EXAMPLE

I'm a lousy mother. I'm always bad tempered with the kids and I don't really want to be with them.

Every mother has times when her children get on her nerves. You can't be perfect all the time. Remember that lovely picnic you took them on two Sundays ago and how you recently spent all your spare time making Jane a pair of trousers and how about when you cancelled your own outing to take them swimming because it had rained all week and they were really fed-up.

Now choose a negative thought of your own and try this exercise in front of a mirror, then record your 'conversation' on the diagram below.

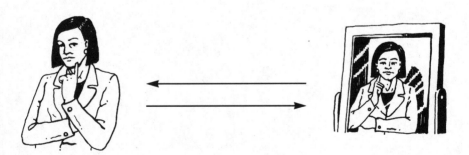

Mirror, Mirror on the Wall

Professional Life
EXAMPLE

I can't get on with my secretary. I'm really mean and snappy with her. I feel such a horrid bitch. I'm sure everyone thinks I'm a real bully.

You've been under a lot of pressure lately, and your secretary does seem to have difficulty taking any initiative herself. Think of all the other colleagues you've helped and how compassionate you are when people have problems. I'm sure they really like and respect you.

Now choose a negative thought of your own and try this exercise in front of a mirror, then record your conversation on the diagram below.

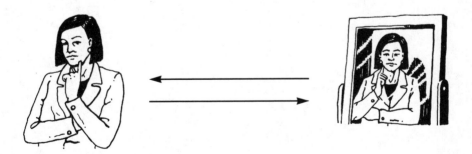

DOUBLE STANDARDS

'Its OK for everyone else but bad if I do it'

The object of both these exercises is to highlight to you that you probably use double standards when dealing with yourself and other people. You would not expect others to be perfect and yet you find it hard to accept and forgive weakness in yourself. You would be compassionate and understanding when dealing with a friend, yet over-critical and unkind to yourself.

Form the habit of talking to yourself as if you really cared and wanted to do the best to help yourself overcome negative thoughts and feelings.

ACCEPT YOUR FAULTS

> '... Grant me the serenity to accept what I can't change,
> the courage to change what I can and the wisdom to know
> the difference'.
>
> ADAPTED FROM REINHOLD NIEBUHR (1943)

The above plea illustrates another method of dealing with negative thoughts and feelings; i.e. acknowledging and accepting them. This method seems very alien to our western culture, but is frequently practised in eastern countries and can be most beneficial.

The philosophy shaping this idea is that you automatically become stronger once you accept the fact that you are weak and flawed. Paradoxically, you become more complete when you acknowledge you are not whole. You experience a real sense of freedom when you stop fighting your negative thoughts and feelings and no longer have to defend or excuse your behaviour.

In the West it is usual for people to resist this form of thinking because we do not want to be seen as 'less than' others. Our culture values strength and perfection and we are unfamiliar with a philosophy that encourages 'gain' through 'loss'. However, if you feel there is some truth in other people's criticism of you echoed in your own self-appraisal, then this technique might help you.

An Example of how this Technique Works

A. Your work is becoming sloppy and you've started missing deadlines.

Normal response

B. It might not be up to my usual standard, but it's certainly as good as most other people's and anyway I've had a lot of pressure at home and I'm feeling under the weather.

Acceptance response

B. You're right, it's well below par. I've missed those deadlines recently.

ACCEPT YOUR FAULTS

Imagine a comment that someone might make to you and which you know would make you defensive, then write it down in the space below. Follow it with a typical response that you would usually make and then write out another response in which you accept the comment calmly and serenely.

COMMENT:

YOUR NORMAL RESPONSE:

ACCEPTANCE RESPONSE:

How did you feel after completing this exercise? Did it make you feel better or worse?

In deciding whether or not to use this method to deal with your negative thoughts and feelings, it is useful to ask yourself whether you felt a sense of release afterwards or even more depressed and hopeless. There are probably times when you need to challenge your negativity in order to feel better, but there will probably also be occasions when calm acceptance is the most beneficial response.

RESPECTING YOURSELF

We know that we truly have good self-esteem when we, ourselves, begin to acknowledge our own strengths. Often we give respect to other people and fail to notice or appreciate our own qualities. Self-respect is vital. Study the following points and after filling them in yourself ask a trusted friend to fill them in as well.

PERSONAL LIFE	WHAT YOU SAY	WHAT YOUR FRIEND SAYS
Any positive relationship or friendship skills that you possess		
Any ways in which you have enhanced your home surroundings		
Any ways that you have communicated your feelings that made you and the other person feel positive		
Any social events that you have organized that went well		
Any books or films you've seen recently that expanded your horizons		
Anyone you have helped recently		
Any letter or phone call you made that demanded a bit of extra courage		
Any exercise or sport that you've tried out recently		

RESPECTING YOURSELF

PERSONAL LIFE	WHAT YOU SAY	WHAT YOUR FRIEND SAYS
Any special hobby/talent you use regularly		
Any organizational change you've initiated in the family set-up which has made people's lives a little easier		
Any contribution you have made to your local community or global welfare		
Any way you handled your children which you are pleased with		
Any other		

RESPECTING YOURSELF

You can ask a trusted colleague to fill in this form after you have completed your section.

PROFESSIONAL LIFE	WHAT YOU SAY	WHAT YOUR COLLEAGUE SAYS
Any piece of work I am particularly proud of		
Any skill that has given me particular success		
Any praise from my colleagues/manager		
Any new challenge I have taken on		
Any time I motivated others		
Any time I interpreted information		
Any other		

RESPECTING YOURSELF

You can ask a trusted colleague to fill in this form after you have completed your section.

PROFESSIONAL LIFE	WHAT YOU SAY	WHAT YOUR COLLEAGUE SAYS
Any task you performed confidently		
Any time I have coped successfully with a dilemma		
Any time I helped or encouraged a colleague who was having work related problems		
Any time I contributed to a new policy or decision		
Any time I took the initiative to make a new proposal		
Any new skill I have learnt		
Any event I have organized		
Any other		

GETTING GOING

Personal Life

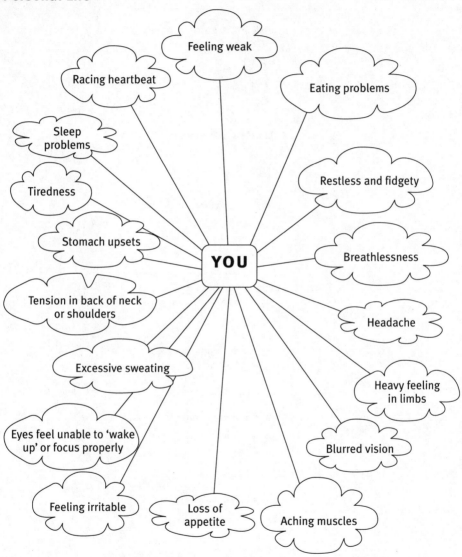

Look at the bubbles and put a ✓ beside three areas where you feel you have low self-esteem and in which you would like to do better. Use the blanks to add any others that are making you anxious or depressed.

GETTING GOING

Personal Life

One successful way of dealing with an area of low self-esteem is to follow a simple and realistic action plan.

Here are six steps which you can apply to each of your areas of concern.

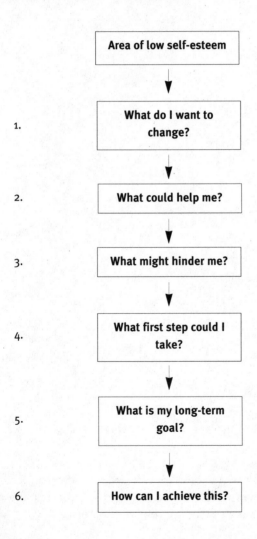

	Area of low self-esteem
1.	**What do I want to change?**
2.	**What could help me?**
3.	**What might hinder me?**
4.	**What first step could I take?**
5.	**What is my long-term goal?**
6.	**How can I achieve this?**

GETTING GOING

Personal Life

Example

Area of low self-esteem
Getting involved in activities outside the home.

1.

What do I want to change?
I'd like to have a better social life and have the
courage to join an amateur dramatic club.

2.

What could help me?
To develop more confidence in myself.

3.

What might hinder me?
Being frightened of meeting new people and
making a fool of myself.

4.

What first step could I take?
Write to the club I want to join and ask them to
send details and an application form.

5.

What is my long-term goal?
To be able to join the club and act. Also, to have
friends with this shared interest.

6.

How can I achieve this?
Actually fill in the application form and send it
off. I could go and watch a few sessions and if
I'm really nervous I could get someone to come
with me.

GETTING GOING

Personal Life

Example

Area of low self-esteem
Trying to please others.

1.

What do I want to change?
I want to be able to please myself sometimes
instead of always doing what others want.

2.

What could help me?
Having a bit more courage.

3.

What might hinder me?
Being afraid of offending people and losing
friends.

4.

What first step could I take?
Saying no to someone I'm fairly sure of.

5.

What is my long-term goal?
To be able to pick and choose whether or not I
want to do what others want or something else.

6.

How can I achieve this?
Read about and practise ways of being
assertive.

GETTING GOING

Personal Life

Complete the next three pages with the areas of low self-esteem you want to improve in your private life.

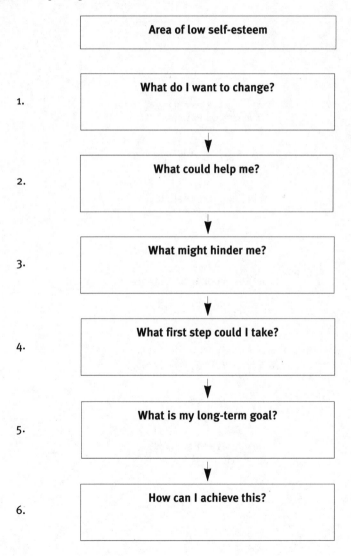

	Area of low self-esteem
1.	**What do I want to change?**
2.	**What could help me?**
3.	**What might hinder me?**
4.	**What first step could I take?**
5.	**What is my long-term goal?**
6.	**How can I achieve this?**

GETTING GOING

Personal Life

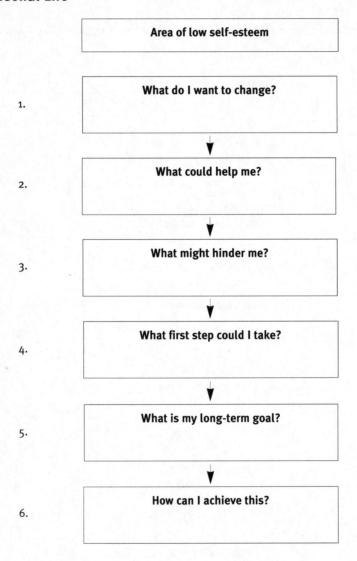

Area of low self-esteem

1.
What do I want to change?

2.
What could help me?

3.
What might hinder me?

4.
What first step could I take?

5.
What is my long-term goal?

6.
How can I achieve this?

GETTING GOING

Professional Life

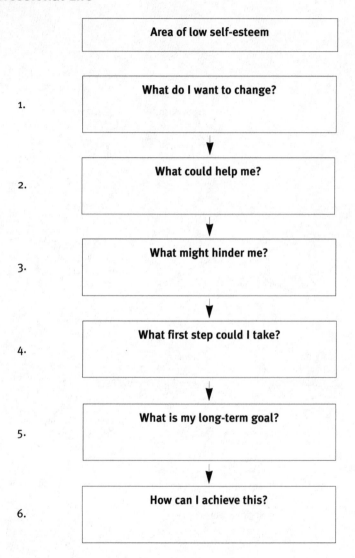

Area of low self-esteem

1. What do I want to change?

2. What could help me?

3. What might hinder me?

4. What first step could I take?

5. What is my long-term goal?

6. How can I achieve this?

GETTING GOING

Professional Life

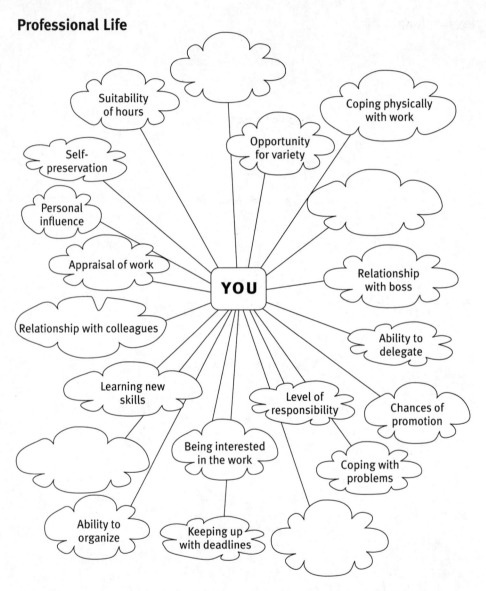

Suitability of hours

Self-preservation

Personal influence

Appraisal of work

Relationship with colleagues

Opportunity for variety

Coping physically with work

YOU

Relationship with boss

Ability to delegate

Learning new skills

Level of responsibility

Chances of promotion

Being interested in the work

Coping with problems

Ability to organize

Keeping up with deadlines

Look at the bubbles and put a ✓ beside three areas where you feel you have low self-esteem and in which you would like to do better. Use the blanks to add any others that are making you anxious or depressed.

GETTING GOING

Professional Life

Example

> **Area of low self-esteem**
> Relationship with boss.

1.
> **What do I want to change?**
> I'd like to be able to chat to her in a more relaxed way.

2.
> **What could help me?**
> To be less nervous and realize she's only another human.

3.
> **What might hinder me?**
> If she thought I was being too forward and pushy.

4.
> **What first step could I take?**
> Before our next meeting I could write down and rehearse *all* I want to say.

5.
> **What is my long-term goal?**
> Not to be at all intimidated so I can show her the best of me.

6.
> **How can I achieve this?**
> Talk more regularly to her. Try and make conversations more 'human'.

GETTING GOING

Professional Life

Example

	Area of low self-esteem Keeping up with deadlines.
1.	**What do I want to change?** Always being stressed to reach deadlines and sometimes late.
2.	**What could help me?** If I could organize my time more efficiently.
3.	**What might hinder me?** Taking on more than I can realistically handle.
4.	**What first step could I take?** Write out a proper time management chart.
5.	**What is my long-term goal?** To be unhurried with assignments. Always have them in on time.
6.	**How can I achieve this?** Stick to writing time management plans. Make sure I'm not being overburdened with too much work.

GETTING GOING

Professional Life

Complete the next three pages with the areas of low self-esteem you want to improve in your professional life.

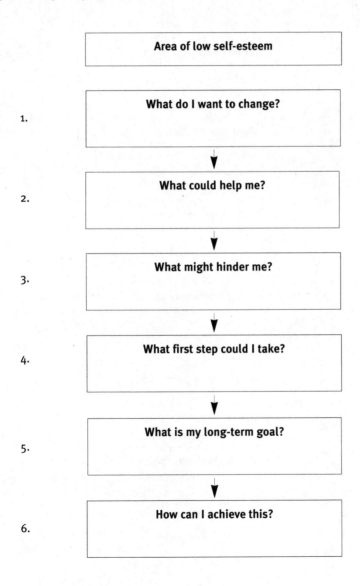

Area of low self-esteem

1. **What do I want to change?**

2. **What could help me?**

3. **What might hinder me?**

4. **What first step could I take?**

5. **What is my long-term goal?**

6. **How can I achieve this?**

GETTING GOING

Professional Life

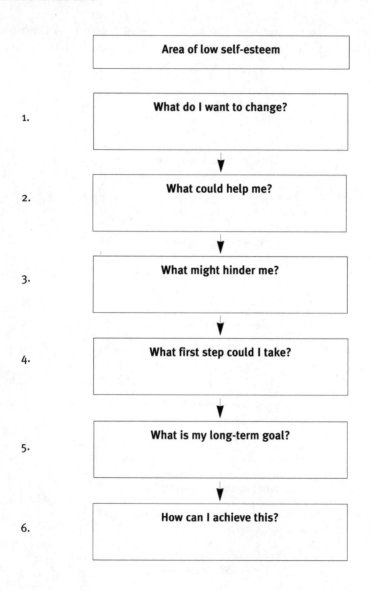

Area of low self-esteem

1. What do I want to change?

2. What could help me?

3. What might hinder me?

4. What first step could I take?

5. What is my long-term goal?

6. How can I achieve this?

GETTING GOING

Professional Life

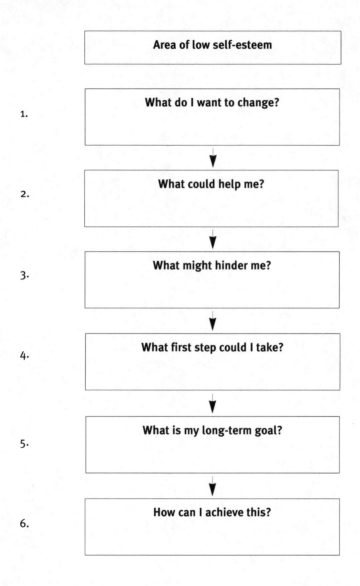

Area of low self-esteem

1. What do I want to change?

2. What could help me?

3. What might hinder me?

4. What first step could I take?

5. What is my long-term goal?

6. How can I achieve this?

Part two

DEALING WITH STRESS

In the previous chapter you will have spent time developing your self-esteem. Consequently, your renewed self-confidence will probably have led you to take on even more challenges. Whilst challenges can be highly motivating and dynamic, nevertheless they can create their own particular stresses and strains. Balancing all the conflicting demands of home and work is a very complex task and most of us suffer, at times, from periods of stress. Stress is a natural condition and part of everyone's life. It can be a healthy force as long as we know how to deal effectively with it. Prolonged stress, however, is emotionally and physically harmful to us and therefore we need to know how to respond positively and recognize when our responses are self-destructive.

THE STRESS RESPONSE

Any physical or emotional threat to your well being can cause a chain of stress responses within you. Adrenaline and cortisones, released by the adrenal glands, stimulate the body to react faster. These physical changes make you feel emotionally charged and anxious.

WHAT HAPPENS	HOW IT PHYSICALLY AFFECTS YOU
Your brain receives a message that you are going to be attacked, either verbally or physically. The adrenal glands are activated. Hormones and chemicals are released into the blood stream.	dry mouth blurred vision
Nerves send messages to various parts of the body to make them ready for action.	breathlessness thumping heart
Airways widen to let in more oxygen and lungs work harder.	butterflies or 'knotted' feeling in stomach
Heart pumps more rapidly to take oxygen and energy to muscles and brain.	agitation
Blood pressure is raised to increase blood volume.	pale skin
Liver releases sugars and fuels into bloodstream.	more frequent need to use toilet
Digestive system slows down to divert energy to muscles.	sweating
Immune system and other systems not necessary for preserving life decline.	aches and pains in muscles
Perspiration occurs to cool muscles.	pins and needles
Muscles tense, ready for action.	
Calcium discharge from tense muscles.	

Any form of confrontation or avoidance action can reduce the tension in your body by using up the extra resources, so that you feel better and 'calmed'. If, however, you are unable to respond to the threat, the chemicals remain in your body for longer and cause discomfort and illness.

> **Example of 'threat':** A sexist comment to you by a senior manager

EFFECTS OF CONTINUAL STRESS

PHYSICAL
- Headaches
- Stomach upsets and ulcers
- Muscle pain
- Furred arteries
- Less immunity to illness
- Tiredness
- Weight loss
- Depressed sensory and mental responses
- Heart disease

COGNITIVE
- Concentration impaired
- Memory span reduced
- Response action reduced
- More errors likely
- Ability to assess and predict accurately reduced
- Thought disorders increased

EMOTIONAL
- Ability to relax reduced
- Emotional outbursts increase
- Personality disorders increase
- Feelings of helplessness increase
- Feelings of worthlessness increase

In order to minimize the harmful effects of too much stress, you must identify the causes of stress in your life and then find ways to alleviate or disperse the physical reactions.

UNDERSTANDING STRESS IN YOUR PRIVATE AND PROFESSIONAL LIFE

This chart estimates the levels of stress induced by the various life events we face. People who have to cope with too many stressful factors at once are more at risk of suffering from health problems. Put a ✓ next to each event which applies to you.

	LIFE EVENT SCORES (ADAPTED FROM HOLMES & RAHE, 1987)	
Death of partner	100	
Divorce	73	
Separation	65	
Death of close member of family	63	
Illness or injury	53	
Marriage	50	
Termination of employment	47	
Reconciliation with spouse	45	
Retirement	45	
Illness in family	45	
Pregnancy	40	
Sexual problems	39	
New family member	39	
Change of work	39	
Financial change	38	
Death of friend	37	
Change of employment	36	

Increasing mortgage	31	
Child leaving home	29	
Conflict with in-laws	29	
Outstanding achievement	28	
Child starting/leaving school	26	
Change of social activities	25	
Conflict with manager	23	
Change of social activities	18	
Change in sleep pattern	16	
Change in eating habits	15	
Holiday	13	
Christmas	12	
	Your total	

Thomas Holmes and Richard Rahe researched the effect of different events on people's health. Their findings showed that for people who had a life event score below 100 there was a 1 in 100 chance of them becoming ill during the next year. The risk increased with the life event score i.e.

Score	Risk of Illness
100–149	3 in 10
150–299	5 in 10
300+	8 in 10

The table was intended to study groups of people and therefore does not take into account individual differences, but it does serve as an indication of how events in our lives can affect our health and well being.

UNDERSTANDING YOUR STRESS PROFILE

What type of person are you? Tick the statements in each box that apply to you.

TYPE A

Very competitive	
Ambitious socially/at work	
Punctual	
Strong, forceful personality	
Impatient	
Walks, moves and eats quickly	
Likes to do several tasks at once	
Easily angered by events or people	
Seeks public recognition	
Has trouble relaxing	
Always rushed	
Few interests outside home/work	
Hides feelings	
Pushes self/others to get things done	

TYPE B

Not competitive	
Happy with present social/work position	
Casual about time-keeping	
Easy-going personality	
Patient	
Walks, moves and eats without rushing	
Concentrates on one task at a time	
Slow to anger	
Not interested in public recognition	
Enjoys periods of relaxation	
Never feels rushed	
Has interests outside home/work	
Is able to show feelings	
Doesn't push self/others to get things done	

Count up how many statements you have ticked in each box and decide whether you are more a type 'A' or type 'B' personality.

If you are a Type A personality you are more likely to suffer from some of the adverse effects of stress i.e. feelings of tension, headaches or illness. Furthermore you might find that you experience problems with your interpersonal relationships and often feel discontented with your life. Type B personalities tend to enjoy better health and experience more satisfaction in their lives, although there can be a tendency for these types to be too 'laid back' and lacking in motivation.

If you are more of a Type A personality you might recognize some of the stress responses that are shown on the following two pages. Make a mental note of how many of these apply to you.

PHYSICAL EFFECTS OF STRESS

Tick, ✓, any of the physical effects that you regularly experience.

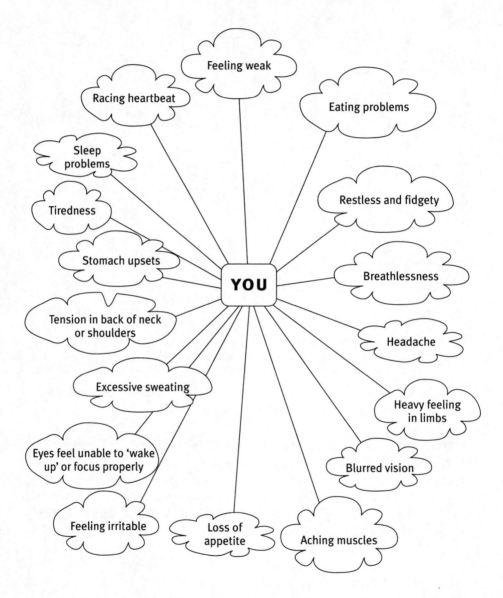

COGNITIVE AND EMOTIONAL EFFECTS OF STRESS

Tick, ✓, any of the cognitive and emotional effects that you regularly experience.

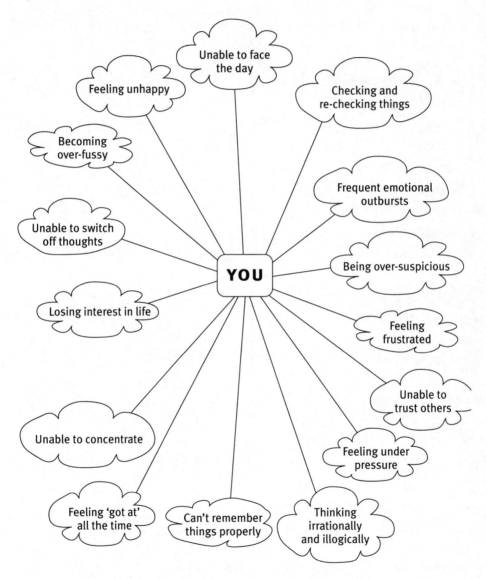

PRIVATE LIFE

How Well are you Coping with Stress?

Look at the list below and circle a number in the scale beside each item to indicate how frequently the item causes you anxiety i.e. (1) never causes you anxiety, (4) sometimes causes you anxiety, (7) always causes you anxiety.

Relationship with your husband/partner	1	2	3	4	5	6	7
Relationship with children	1	2	3	4	5	6	7
Organizing shopping	1	2	3	4	5	6	7
Preparing meals	1	2	3	4	5	6	7
Keeping house together	1	2	3	4	5	6	7
Seeing relatives	1	2	3	4	5	6	7
Selecting your clothes	1	2	3	4	5	6	7
Keeping healthy	1	2	3	4	5	6	7
Developing spiritual self	1	2	3	4	5	6	7
Sleeping properly	1	2	3	4	5	6	7
Finding time alone	1	2	3	4	5	6	7
Making time for hobbies	1	2	3	4	5	6	7
Decorating	1	2	3	4	5	6	7
Organizing social life	1	2	3	4	5	6	7
Maintaining friendships	1	2	3	4	5	6	7
Financial security	1	2	3	4	5	6	7
Holidays	1	2	3	4	5	6	7
Car Problems	1	2	3	4	5	6	7
Gardening	1	2	3	4	5	6	7
Neighbours	1	2	3	4	5	6	7

Add together all the numbers you have circled and write down your total score.

Total Score ☐

Well done! You are coping well with all the stress factors in you life. Just make sure that you are looking after yourself and giving yourself sufficient treats.

Despite all the stresses that are affecting you, you are managing to keep things in perspective. Some things seem to be out of your control and you do need to learn positive coping responses for specific areas in your life.

Things really get on top of you. Life must feel like an upward battle with little time for relaxation and peace of mind. Your coping responses are negative and ineffective. You deserve better from life and must start to take stress management more seriously before your emotional and physical health deteriorates.

20–60

61–100

101–140

PROFESSIONAL LIFE

How Well are you Coping with Stress?

Look at the list below and circle a number in the scale beside each item to indicate how frequently the item causes you anxiety i.e. (1) never causes you anxiety, (4) sometimes causes you anxiety, (7) always causes you anxiety.

Physical surroundings/temperature	1	2	3	4	5	6	7
Contact with management	1	2	3	4	5	6	7
Contact with colleagues	1	2	3	4	5	6	7
Overlong working hours	1	2	3	4	5	6	7
Meeting deadlines	1	2	3	4	5	6	7
Using technology/equipment	1	2	3	4	5	6	7
Work encroaching on personal time (e.g. lunch breaks, evenings, weekends)	1	2	3	4	5	6	7
Sexual harassment	1	2	3	4	5	6	7
Undefined objectives	1	2	3	4	5	6	7
Poor instructions	1	2	3	4	5	6	7
Making decisions	1	2	3	4	5	6	7
Poor eating/drinking habits at work	1	2	3	4	5	6	7
Sexual/racial discrimination	1	2	3	4	5	6	7
Taking on extra work (e.g. through colleague's absence)	1	2	3	4	5	6	7
Punctuality	1	2	3	4	5	6	7
Lack of interest in your work	1	2	3	4	5	6	7
Lack of support from management	1	2	3	4	5	6	7
Lack of promotion	1	2	3	4	5	6	7
Fitting in your holiday	1	2	3	4	5	6	7
Company performance	1	2	3	4	5	6	7

Add together all the numbers you have circled and write down your total score.

Total Score

Great! You are managing to cope very well at work. Your ability to deal with stress is good. Are you sure, however, that you are meeting new challenges and have important goals to reach. You have great potential, make sure that you use it fully.

20–60

Despite the stress that you have to cope with at work you are managing to do a good job. Occasionally, however, you do let things get on top of you. Because you do not manage these situations as well, you are not doing yourself justice or presenting yourself as successfully as you could.

61–100

Things are obviously affecting you far too much. Are you sure you are in the right job? If you think you are, then you must concentrate on developing your positive stress responses in order to have any career satisfaction.

101–140

NEGATIVE OR POSITIVE RESPONSES

When we are faced with an emotional, cognitive or physical threat, we respond by altering our emotions and behaviour in order to cope. If these adjustments are inadequate or inappropriate, they will not deal effectively with the cause of our stress and it will continue to trouble us. In these circumstances the harmful physical effects of stress are prolonged by the negative coping strategies that we have adopted. We have to make sure that our coping responses have positive results.

Example
Private Life

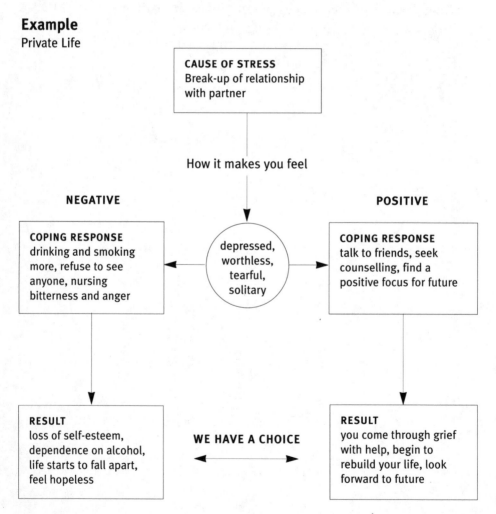

CAUSE OF STRESS
Break-up of relationship with partner

How it makes you feel

NEGATIVE

COPING RESPONSE
drinking and smoking more, refuse to see anyone, nursing bitterness and anger

depressed, worthless, tearful, solitary

POSITIVE

COPING RESPONSE
talk to friends, seek counselling, find a positive focus for future

RESULT
loss of self-esteem, dependence on alcohol, life starts to fall apart, feel hopeless

WE HAVE A CHOICE

RESULT
you come through grief with help, begin to rebuild your life, look forward to future

NEGATIVE OR POSITIVE RESPONSES

Example
Professional Life

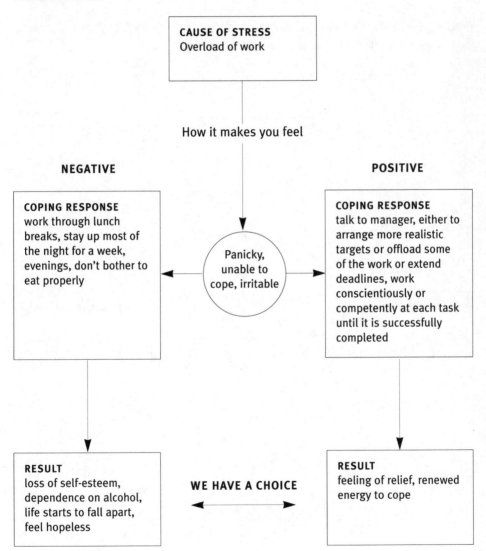

CAUSE OF STRESS
Overload of work

How it makes you feel

NEGATIVE

POSITIVE

COPING RESPONSE
work through lunch
breaks, stay up most of
the night for a week,
evenings, don't bother to
eat properly

Panicky,
unable to
cope, irritable

COPING RESPONSE
talk to manager, either to
arrange more realistic
targets or offload some
of the work or extend
deadlines, work
conscientiously or
competently at each task
until it is successfully
completed

RESULT
loss of self-esteem,
dependence on alcohol,
life starts to fall apart,
feel hopeless

WE HAVE A CHOICE

RESULT
feeling of relief, renewed
energy to cope

NEGATIVE OR POSITIVE RESPONSES

Professional Life
Example

Repeat the process with a situation from your professional life that you have not dealt with effectively in the past or the present.

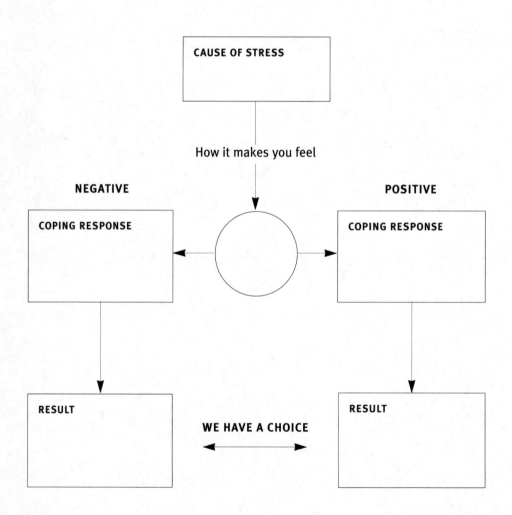

NEGATIVE OR POSITIVE RESPONSES

Private Life
Example

Now choose a situation from your private life, either past or present, which you have not coped well with and which either continued or continues to trouble you. Fill in the boxes below and see how you could have dealt effectively with the situation by choosing a positive coping response.

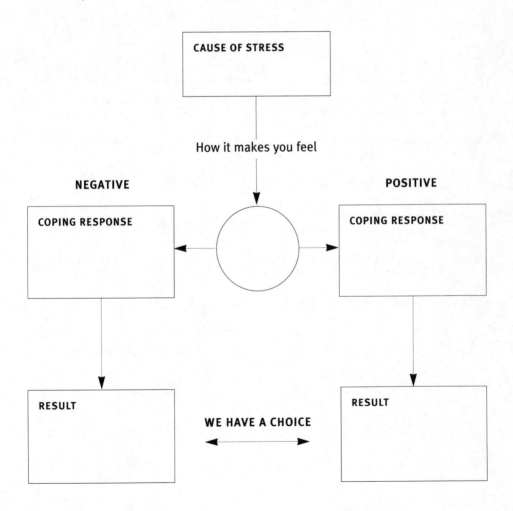

RECOGNIZING NEGATIVE RESPONSES

Personal Life
Kate's Day

Below is a typical day in the life of Kate. As you read through it, note down in the boxes by the side, some of the negative responses that she makes, how this makes her feel and how she might change these responses and feelings to positive ones. The example will show you how to do this.

NEGATIVE RESPONSE	NEGATIVE FEELING	POSITIVE RESPONSE	POSITIVE FEELING
Example Anger at child for disturbing her	resent-ment, guilt	'Hello sweetheart. It's too early to play. Why don't you go and get teddy dressed and tell him a story?'	No guilt, Kate has resolved the situation without upsetting her daughter.

It is 7.30 a.m. on Sunday morning. Kate's three year-old daughter, Amy, bounces into her bedroom wanting to play. *'Go back to bed,'* shouts Kate angrily, *'it's too early.'* The little girl's happy face crumples in rejection; miserably she shuffles back to her own bedroom. Ten minutes later the child returns to repeat her request. *'Ask daddy,'* moans Kate. Amy walks around the bed to her father and begins to poke him asking him to play with her. He groans and dives underneath the bedclothes saying *'Talk to mummy, I'm tired.'* Kate feels angry and resentful. She now pokes John, *'Why can't you get up and see to Amy for a change?'* she challenges. *'It's Sunday,'* John responds. *'I have to get up early for work every day. I want to lie in on Sunday.'*

'What about **my** *Sunday?'* Kate shouts. *'When do I have a Sunday to lie in? You never take your fair share. She's your child as well.'* Amy begins to cry. Kate flings off the bedclothes and leaps out of bed. She grabs Amy's hand and drags her out of the room and down to the kitchen. *'Shut up,'* she says harshly. The child cries even more.

NEGATIVE RESPONSE	NEGATIVE FEELING	POSITIVE RESPONSE	POSITIVE FEELING

Kate prepares Amy's breakfast; all the while her resentment against John builds *'No-one is ever interested in my needs,'* she mutters to herself.

Some time later John appears. He is obviously being nice to Kate to try and placate her and make amends. Kate, however, refuses to respond. She either ignores John or snaps at him.

'Would you like to go and see your sister this morning?' he asks her.

'No, I wouldn't,' Kate snarls. *'I've far too much to do and I'm not going to get any help from anyone am I?'*

'Oh well, please yourself,' says John. He is beginning to get fed up with her bad mood.

After breakfast he says, *'I'm going out to wash the car.'*

'Oh that's right,' snaps Kate, *'clear off outside, leave me and Amy as usual. It might have been nice if you'd offered to do something for us.'*

Now John is angry. *'If you think I'm going to stay in with you being such a pain you're mistaken. In fact, I shall go down the pub when I've finished.'* *'Oh yes,'* Kate is sarcastic, *'run away to your stupid cronies. You're all the same, selfish! Well, don't expect any dinner when you get back, because I shan't cook you any.'*

When John has gone, Kate feels really miserable. She thinks how often similar, small incidents escalate into major rows.

NEGATIVE RESPONSE	NEGATIVE FEELING	POSITIVE RESPONSE	POSITIVE FEELING

'It's all my fault,' she thinks. *'If I wasn't so bad-tempered this wouldn't have happened. I could have made it alright again, but I didn't.'*

Kate's neighbour, Sue, calls in for a coffee. She looks happy and radiant which makes Kate feel worse. Kate tells her that she and John have rowed again. *'Oh, I'm so glad Pete and I get on well. I couldn't stand all the hassle of rows,'* Sue responds. *'Self-satisfied cow,'* thinks Kate. *'She reckons she's so superior to me.'* *'Pete and I are going to a car boot sale. Do you want to come with us and see if you can get any bargains?'* Sue asks. The idea appeals to Kate, but her injured pride and misery make her refuse. She knows the outing would make her feel better but she wants to hang onto her resentment as she is not ready to forgive John.

She is also cross with Sue for seeming to manage her life better and wants to hurt her.

'Are you putting on a bit of weight?' she asks spitefully. Sue does not reply.

Kate feels full of remorse when Sue has left, *'why did I behave so meanly to her?'* she asks herself. *'She's so nice and I'm such a bitch. It's no wonder I have so many problems. I deserve them!'*

The day drags boringly on. Kate feels lonely. She decides that she will be pleasant to John when he does get home, so that the rest of the day can be salvaged. However, when John does return he has brought home a friend for moral support.

NEGATIVE RESPONSE	NEGATIVE FEELING	POSITIVE RESPONSE	POSITIVE FEELING

Kate is instantly furious. She feels as if John has messed up her plans intentionally. *'What's he doing here?'* she hisses to John in the hall. *'He's going to help me in the garden this afternoon,'* John replies. Kate explodes, *'after your selfish behaviour this morning, the least you could do is try to make amends by taking me and Amy out.'*

'Me selfish?' shouts back John. *'You're the one who's selfish.'* *'Well, I'm going out then,'* Kate says.

She slams out of the house and strides down the road. She has nowhere she wants to go. She doesn't want to visit anyone and see them happy, so she spends several hours just wandering around, rather than go back home. She begins to feel cold, but her anger prevents her from returning home. Her thoughts alternate between self-pity and self-loathing. They become distorted and exaggerated leaving her confused and miserable.

When she does at last return home, John is on the settee watching the television. Amy is curled up beside him playing with her dolls. They look companionable and contented.

'They'd probably be better off without me,' thinks Kate. Self-pity fuels her bad mood so that she cannot let go of her anger and resentment. She makes tea for them all and deliberately burns John's toast. This small act of spite does not make her feel any better. *'Let's play boats,'* says Amy to her as she bathes the child. *'Oh, I'm too tired,'* Kate answers. *'You're a*

NEGATIVE RESPONSE	NEGATIVE FEELING	POSITIVE RESPONSE	POSITIVE FEELING

spoilsport,' says the little girl.

Stung by this remark, Kate snaps. *'If you'd had a hard day like I have you wouldn't feel like playing either.'*

Amy sulks and refuses to kiss Kate goodnight. As she looks at her small daughter in bed, Kate is overwhelmed by feelings of inadequacy. *'I'm such a bad mother,'* she thinks. *'My poor little girl will grow up with so many hang-ups and problems.'*

Kate feels that she can't cope with much more. She goes downstairs hoping to have a chat with John and regain some peace in her life, but when she sees him still watching the television, her resentment mounts again. *'He doesn't even care,'* she thinks, *'he must see how unhappy I am, but it doesn't bother him. All he's interested in is himself.'*

Instead of talking to John, Kate climbs the stairs to her bedroom and goes to bed where she cries herself to sleep.

CHANGING NEGATIVE TO POSITIVE

Emma's Day

Now look through Emma's day at work and see if it is possible to change her negative responses to positive ones.

NEGATIVE RESPONSE	NEGATIVE FEELING	POSSIBLE POSITIVE RESPONSE	POSSIBLE POSITIVE FEELING
turning volume up to annoy her neighbour	resentful, angry, mean, guilty	turns volume down, pleased to oblige and avoid confront-ation	calm and in control

Emma is awake, as is usual recently, at 5.00 a.m. She has had problems sleeping properly for several weeks now. She switches on her radio to loud music and lights a cigarette. After ten minutes, the woman in the next flat bangs on the wall, disturbed by the music. Emma turns up the volume, knowing she will complain to the landlord, but not caring.

When she gathers up her bits for work, she notices that she's left coffee rim stains over an important report that her manager needed that morning. *'Oh damn!"* wails Emma, *'what am I going to do now?'* Emma spends ten minutes trying to wipe off the stain but just makes the paper crumpled and muddy looking. She is late leaving the house, so arrives at work hot, flustered and irritable.

'Good morning, Emma,' Sally, the receptionist, greets her with a friendly smile. Emma hardly responds and rushes past. *'Oh hell,'* she thinks, *'I suppose she is going to get in a twist now. Still, I haven't got time to go back and explain.'*

NEGATIVE RESPONSE	NEGATIVE FEELING	POSSIBLE POSITIVE RESPONSE	POSSIBLE POSITIVE FEELING

As Emma is about to enter her office, she sees her manager standing by her desk. Emma rushes off to hide in the loo. She smokes a quick cigarette. Someone comes in and expresses disgust at the smoky room. *'There's no damn notice against smoking in here,'* states Emma defiantly.

When she emerges from the ladies, her manager has disappeared. *'He will now think I am late for work.'* She is so agitated about the ruined report she now feels a headache starting. She is tired from lack of sleep and feels unable to concentrate.

Glancing abstractedly through the morning's mail, she notices there is an invitation to a workshop, outlining recent innovations in informational technology which she should attend. *'Oh, blow that, far too boring,'* she mutters and flings it into the wastepaper bin.

The mid-morning tea trolley comes round. Emma chooses a large fresh cream cake, although she is already slightly overweight and fed up that clothes are beginning to feel uncomfortable. *'What does it matter?'* she thinks gloomily. *'Anyway, I need cheering up.'* After eating she feels slight indigestion and guilty about the excess calories.

Unable to tackle her work immediately she stands by the window watching the traffic. *'I wish I was off doing something exciting,'* she reflects, *'what am I doing in this dump anyway?'*

NEGATIVE RESPONSE	NEGATIVE FEELING	POSSIBLE POSITIVE RESPONSE	POSSIBLE POSITIVE FEELING

At this moment her manager walks in. *'I can see you're overworked, Emma,'* he comments. *'I've just stopped by to pick up your report. I did call in around nine, but you hadn't arrived then.'*

Emma feels herself blushing. She cannot look him in the eye. *'I'm sure I put it on your desk yesterday afternoon,'* she says trying to look bright and confident, *'you weren't around, so I left it on your desk. Perhaps someone's moved it.'* Looking at her quizzically, he said *'I'll ask around.'* He leaves the office. Emma feels dreadful. She knows this lie will lead to others, as she'll have to find a way of returning the report tomorrow after she has re-done the messy pages. She will probably lose his trust, so there will definitely be no chance for promotion now. Her head is really throbbing. In an effort to work through her 'mood', Emma dashes off several letters. They are badly worded and slip-shod, but Emma sends them off to the typist anyway. She knows that her standards are slipping and that people will begin to see her as unreliable and uncommitted, but she is so tired lately and cannot find any enthusiasm for her work. At lunch time, she turns down the offer of a stroll in the park in favour of a burger and chips in the canteen. The noise and smells of the canteen make her headache so bad that she is almost sick with the pain.

Emma struggles inefficiently through the afternoon. Steve, from the next office, pops in at 5.30 p.m. to invite her to the pub with several other colleagues. It

NEGATIVE RESPONSE	NEGATIVE FEELING	POSSIBLE POSITIVE RESPONSE	POSSIBLE POSITIVE FEELING

would be good to swap work news with them and relax with them over a pint, but Emma has to re-do her report and feels too shoddy after her day.

'What have I got in common with them?' she thinks, *'I'm an incompetent fraud.'* 'Sorry Steve,' she says, *'I've got to meet my mother.'*

Another lie adds to her feelings of guilt.

She could do with talking to someone about her problems, but feels too ashamed of her behaviour to admit it to anyone. Dejectedly, she sets off home to her report, her irate neighbour and another night of broken sleep.

NEGATIVE V POSITIVE COPING RESPONSES

NEGATIVE **POSITIVE**

| Denying a problem exists in the hope it will disappear. | ← **?** → | Acknowledge the problem and find an effective way to deal with it. |

| Finding comfort in smoking, drinking or drug abuse. | ← **?** → | Try 'laughter' as a tonic; go out with friends for a fun evening – see a live comedy show. |

| Eating for comfort or developing other eating disorders. | ← **?** → | Join a self-help group or seek individual counselling help. |

| Making excuses for your own or other people's behaviour. | ← **?** → | Understand you are doing this because it seems the easier option. Face up to reality and be willing to change. |

| Behaving obsessively. | ← **?** → | Find a way to dissipate negative feelings and put problem into perspective. |

| Substituting the real cause of stress for a less threatening target. | ← **?** → | Have the courage to identify and face up to the real problem. Ask people for their view of your situation. |

| Trying to change your personality to fit in with other people's wishes. | ← **?** → | Respect who you are, and find ways to raise your self-esteem. |

| Moaning to other people about your problems. | ← **?** → | Discuss problems with someone who can give valid advice. |

NEGATIVE   **POSITIVE**

Blaming other people for your failures.	◄ ? ►	Learn to forgive yourself for mistakes so you do not have to shift blame from yourself.
Irrational temper outbursts or mood swings.	◄ ? ►	Learn relaxation techniques. Learn to breathe properly. Talk positively to yourself.
Rushing from one coping strategy to another.	◄ ? ►	Take time, consider all options and adopt only those which will be effective. Make small realistic targets.
Developing psychosomatic illness.	◄ ? ►	Identify cause of stress. Check with doctor.
Preferring fantasy to reality.	◄ ? ►	Find ways to make the reality worth living.
Allowing feelings of regret over past bad choices to prevent future fulfilment.	◄ ? ►	Learn to live with mistakes and make the best of chances for the future.

MAKING POSITIVE RESPONSES

Personal Life

Choose some areas of stress from your private life where you could achieve success, if you made changes to your coping responses.

NEGATIVE COPING RESPONSE AND WHAT EFFECT IT HAS ON YOUR LIFE	ALTERNATIVE POSITIVE COPING RESPONSE AND HOW THIS MIGHT ACHIEVE SUCCESS
Example My husband won't look after the children so that I can go to evening class. I feel resentful, so I always find reasons why he can't go out on his own and enjoy himself.	**Example** Suggest to my husband that we use a baby-sitter and both go out on the same evening to an event of our choice.

PROFESSIONAL LIFE

Now do the same for areas of stress in your professional life.

NEGATIVE COPING RESPONSE AND WHAT EFFECT IT HAS ON YOUR LIFE	ALTERNATIVE POSITIVE COPING RESPONSE AND HOW THIS MIGHT ACHIEVE SUCCESS
Example Inefficiency over paperwork. I hate doing it and leave it to pile up, then I panic, it all gets muddled and it takes me ages to sort out.	**Example** Set allotted days and times each week to tackle paperwork, with a reward for sticking to them. Think of a bigger reward to give myself after a month of success.

TAKING ACTION

Three Steps to Dealing with Stress

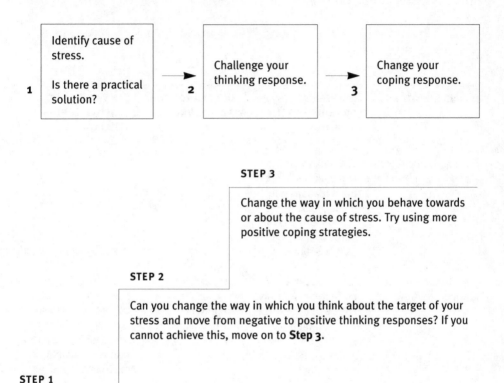

STEP 3

Change the way in which you behave towards or about the cause of stress. Try using more positive coping strategies.

STEP 2

Can you change the way in which you think about the target of your stress and move from negative to positive thinking responses? If you cannot achieve this, move on to **Step 3.**

STEP 1

Find out what the root cause of your stress is and see if there is an obvious practical solution to either remove the cause or remove yourself from it. If not move on to **Step 2.**

TAKING ACTION

Personal Life
The Three Step Action Plan

CAUSE OF STRESS	1 IS THERE AN OBVIOUS PRACTICAL SOLUTION?	2 CAN I CHANGE THE WAY I THINK?	3 CAN I USE MORE POSITIVE COPING STRATEGIES?
I'm getting deeper and deeper into debt	Yes. Talk to my bank manager and work out a realistic and manageable schedule to pay off debts over an agreed length of time.		
My friends are always 'putting on' me.	No. I just can't say no to them. It always comes out the wrong way and then they get upset with me, so now I just put up with all their demands.	I just don't know how I can be different, because they're used to the way I am.	Yes. I could study how to be assertive so that I can refuse their demands in a firm positive way that won't damage my friendships.
I have to organize a social event for our local women's group and I'm terrified it won't be up to the usual standard.	No. I can't get out of doing it and I don't want to ask any of the others for help as they all do them on their own. I want to be seen as being as capable as they are.	Yes. I can stop being frightened and look on this as a challenge which will bring me personal satisfaction and a sense of achievement.	

TAKING ACTION

Personal Life
Using the Three Step Action Plan

Choose areas of stress in your private life and follow the three step plan.

	1	2	3
CAUSE OF STRESS	IS THERE AN OBVIOUS PRACTICAL SOLUTION?	CAN I CHANGE THE WAY I THINK?	CAN I USE MORE POSITIVE COPING STRATEGIES?

TAKING ACTION

Professional Life
Examples of Three Step Action Plan

	1	2	3
CAUSE OF STRESS	IS THERE AN OBVIOUS PRACTICAL SOLUTION?	CAN I CHANGE THE WAY I THINK?	CAN I USE MORE POSITIVE COPING STRATEGIES?
I'm not going to have this piece of work completed by the deadline.	Yes. I can talk to my manager and ask for more time.		
I hate writing out my monthly report. It gives me so much hassle. I just don't enjoy doing that sort of work.	No. It has to be done. I can't avoid it.	Yes. I can see it as a 'necessary' evil, by talking to myself about the positive reasons for doing the monthly report I can learn to hate it less. I can also give myself a treat if I tackle it more positively next time.	
I am being sexually harassed by a chap at work.	No. I just couldn't bring myself to make a complaint. I'm too frightened of the consequences.	No. I feel really degraded and 'used'.	Yes. I could learn positive techniques of working off the man's advances. I could join a self-help or support group to learn how to do this and give me the courage to carry it through. I'd be happier to do it this way and avoid involving other people at work.

TAKING ACTION

Professional Life
Using the Three Step Plan

	1	2	3
CAUSE OF STRESS	IS THERE AN OBVIOUS PRACTICAL SOLUTION?	CAN I CHANGE THE WAY I THINK?	CAN I USE MORE POSITIVE COPING STRATEGIES?

NEGATIVE OR POSITIVE RESPONSE

Negative Responses Increase Stress
Positive Responses Reduce Stress

Causes of Stress

family pressures	social pressure	death of someone	discrimination
work pressures	ill health	close	harassment
emotional pressures	poor living	pain	
financial pressures	conditions	making decisions	
	coping with change	phobias	

Negative responses can increase stress and lead to emotional and physical deterioration.

tiredness, depression, emotional outbursts, tension pains, anxiety, eating disorders, illness, lack of concentration, drug or alcohol abuse, insomnia, irritability, losing trust.

exhaustion, nervous breakdown, instability, chronic ill health, dependence on drugs or alcohol, psychosomatic illness, being obsessive

breakdown in relationships, physical collapse, inability to cope with future, stress, prolonged mental illness, loss of happiness, lack of personal fulfilment

Positive responses lead to an effective reduction of stress and return to well-being.

positive thinking, healthy eating, seeking counselling, efficient use of time, positive physical enhancement, learning self-help techniques, ability to change circumstances

better physical health, mental and emotional well-being, increased self-confidence

enhanced relationships, physical well-being, ability to cope with future stress, mental well-being, increased happiness, greater fulfilment

STRESS PROOFING

You can enhance your ability to cope with stress by becoming prepared both mentally and physically.

You have read about the physical and emotional effects of stress, and how to deal positively with them. You can increase your level of success if you work on being healthy in your mind and body.

Physical Fitness

A fit healthy body is better able to cope with the chemical changes that occur as a result of stress responses. Regular exercise improves the efficiency of the heart, reduces blood pressure and blood sugar levels, helps keep joints flexible and releases muscle tension. Exercise also increases your energy levels so that you have more stamina in your everyday life.

Diet

Stress induced chemicals can, if they remain in the body for too long, cause physical impairment and disorders such as hardening of the arteries, heart disease, and kidney damage. If you add to this too many toxic substances through a diet of excess fat, sugar, and junk food and insufficient vitamins and minerals you are greatly increasing the risk of illness. It is important that your diet is well balanced and contains sufficient quantities of the following nutritional elements.

- Protein
- Carbohydrates
- Vitamins
- Minerals
- Fats

- Eat plenty of fresh fruit and vegetables.
- Replace some tea, coffee and cola with fresh fruit juices or water.
- Make sure you eat sufficient fibre to aid digestion.
- Choose healthier alternatives to frying.

Relaxation

Relaxation is a useful way of freeing the muscles from tension. Learning relaxation techniques will allow you to assess when your body is tense and to really feel the difference between tense and relaxed muscle. Relaxation exercises should not simply be used at certain allocated times, but at any time of the day that you feel stressed and under pressure, so that you can consciously release the tension as soon as it arises.

This exercise is a useful short programme. Practise it at home initially in quiet surroundings seated in a comfortable armchair. When you have mastered the technique use it in everyday circumstances when you feel stressed.

Breathe in and out slowly.
Sigh on the out-breaths and be aware that you are releasing the tension from your body.
Repeat this several times then return to normal breathing.
Concentrate your attention onto your forehead. 'Feel' it growing wider, feel your eyes sink deep into their sockets, let your cheeks soften and your jaw relax.
Think of a smile on your face.
Now relax your shoulders, feel them drop.
Concentrate on your right arm and hand – feel the tension flow down your arm and out of your fingertips; allow them to relax and soften.
Repeat this for your left arm and hand.
Now become aware of your body, feel it growing softer and more relaxed.
Travel in your mind down your right leg to your right foot.
Feel the tension being released through your toes, feel your foot grow warm and heavy.
Repeat this for your left leg and foot.
Now that your body is relaxed concentrate on each breath and feel a sensation of peace flowing into you, feel yourself drifting in the gentle calmness surrounding you.
When you have enjoyed this sensation for several minutes you can gradually and gently bring your consciousness back to the present.
Open your eyes and stretch your whole body and then 'let go'.
Repeat this a few times.

MENTAL FITNESS

Meditation

The aim of meditation is to increase 'awareness' by focusing attention on a single object or experience. It helps us to:

1) train our attention
2) increase our control over our thought processes
3) learn how to deal effectively with our emotions

Stress is often experienced because of the negative thought processes we have. Sometimes, we repeatedly go over in our minds a bad event that has happened to us; we simply cannot let go of the event and the feelings it aroused. Because of this, we continue to experience the stress aroused by the event and we also prevent ourselves from enjoying other good experiences.

Alternatively, we often become stressed thinking about a bad event that might happen to us in the future and how it would make us feel. Again, the event can so monopolize our thoughts and emotions that we are unable to focus on and enjoy any good events that do occur.

If we could learn to put aside bad experiences, to see them as a learning process from which we can gain valuable insight and discard the negativity that is initially aroused, we would not only release the stress involved, but we would also free ourselves to enjoy good experiences.

Similarly, if we could learn to stop agonizing over events that might not necessarily happen we could also free our minds and emotions to enjoy positive experiences.

In other words, we must learn to live for the experience of the moment and not to dwell on past unhappiness or future anxieties.

Meditation helps us to achieve this by training the mind, so that we can exercise more control over our thoughts. We can choose what we will think about and what we will discard as negative and harmful to our mental and emotional well-being. There are many books and local groups which will instruct you on meditation and how to use it to reduce stress levels.

Sleep

Lack of sleep can increase the effects of stress by undermining our ability to cope. Sleep has long been known to have a therapeutic effect on our minds and bodies and sleep deprivation has been used as a form of torture. Without quality sleep we become listless, depressed, irrational and over emotional.

If you are experiencing prolonged lack of sleep or disturbed sleep then it would be wise to seek medical advice. There are certain simple groundrules that you can observe to aid sleep:

- Avoid stimulants like coffee, alcohol and cigarettes late at night.
- Don't eat a meal prior to going to bed.
- Switch off mental activity such as 'homework' at least half an hour before bedtime.
- Distract yourself from worries with a book, the television or meditation.
- Try to establish a regular routine of sleep time.
- Don't go to bed until you are tired.
- If you can't sleep, don't lie in bed fretting, get up and have a milky drink, read a book or watch television for a while.

Spiritual Well-Being

Many people find that religious beliefs give them the inner resources and faith to cope with stressful situations. Fellow 'believers' also provide a self-help or support group to offer counselling and advice. It is a real source of inspiration and hope to know that a supreme, spiritual being cares about you and can offer you help and understanding throughout the crises in your life.

Keep a Diary – Help stress-proof yourself by keeping a diary. Try to make entries in an objective, unemotional way.

Stress Diary *Rating:* 1. Very positive day 2. Positive day 3. Average day 4. Difficult day 5. Very stressed day

Day	Date	Something I achieved A positive event A positive conversation	Stress factors that occurred	Rating for the day	Reasons for the evaluation
Monday					
Tuesday					
Wednesday					
Thursday					
Friday					
Saturday					
Sunday					

EMERGENCY COPING STRATEGIES

You can also stress-proof yourself by learning to use emergency coping strategies at times of crisis, to prevent the stress response from being activated or to lessen its effect.

Use Emergency Coping Strategies

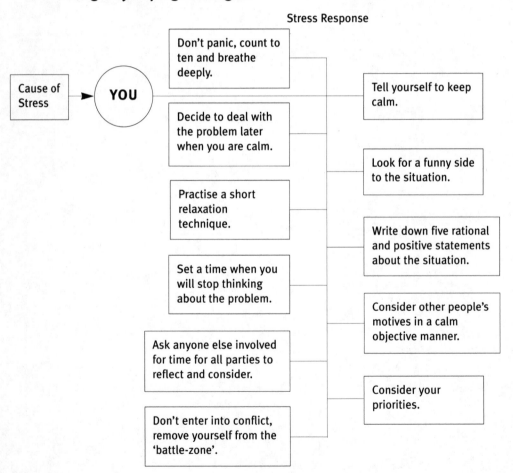

Part three

Developing Assertive Behaviour

Assertiveness forms a major part of this workbook as it is such an important interpersonal skill. Your ability to behave assertively affects everything you do or don't do, from dealing with everyday activities to making major life decisions. Much non-assertive behaviour has its source in low self-esteem. The earlier sections of the workbook showed that low self-esteem may trap you in a negative belief cycle which frequently leads to stress and anxiety in many situations. Very often the worry about situations or events comes to include everything connected with them, particularly the people involved. In your anxiety to cope, you may resort to non-assertive behaviour. The quality of your personal and professional relationships is likely to deteriorate as a result.

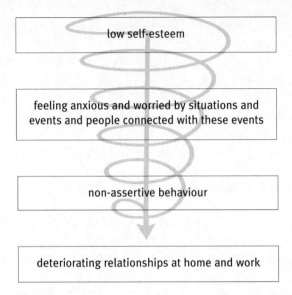

low self-esteem

feeling anxious and worried by situations and
events and people connected with these events

non-assertive behaviour

deteriorating relationships at home and work

Learning to behave assertively is essential if you want to improve your
personal effectiveness. This section builds up an understanding of
assertiveness and offers practical suggestions for developing your own
assertive skills in your personal and professional relationships.

Some of the benefits which may result from behaving more assertively are
listed overleaf. Read through the list and identify why you want to improve
your assertive skills.

By behaving assertively:

☑ your confidence in yourself increases.

☑ you allow others to really understand you.

☑ you will feel better for saying how you feel.

☑ you are more open to people letting you know how they feel.

☑ your relationships are based on truth and reality.

☑ you will not be afraid to take risks.

☑ you will be able to accept your own strengths and weaknesses.

☑ even if things don't improve you'll feel better for having tried.

I want to improve my assertive skills because:

WHAT IS ASSERTIVENESS?

There is considerable confusion surrounding the term 'assertiveness', so it is important to clarify the meaning for yourself and distinguish assertive behaviour from aggressive, manipulative and passive behaviour.

Write down your own definition for each of these behaviours below. Think quickly. Don't bother to write down sentences. Jot down anything and everything which comes to mind including body language, vocabulary used, people you know who behave in this way, and how they make you feel.

Being aggressive means:

Being manipulative means:

Being passive means:

Being assertive means:

Compare your own definition with the descriptions below:

Aggressive behaviour is:

- being loud and abusive.
- winning at any cost to other people.
- getting your own way by force or threat.
- forcing others to do things they don't want to do.
- causing others to feel hurt, resentful, humiliated or put down.

vocabulary: if you don't, I insist, idiot! you'd better ...
body language: pointing finger, loud voice, shouting, folded arms, staring

---

Manipulative behaviour is:

- being indirectly aggressive and hurtful.
- making people feel small.
- using sarcastic comments.
- tricking others or deceiving people.
- sulking or ignoring people.
- smiling and being polite on the surface while harbouring
  resentment underneath.

vocabulary: I didn't mean to, I meant to tell you, everybody says you ... ,
                  even a child knows how to ... , I think you ought to know
body language: pouting expression, deliberate turning away, resigned
                  expression, scowl, shrugging shoulders, half smile

---

Passive behaviour is:

- always putting yourself down.
- opting out and avoiding confrontation.
- saying 'yes' when you mean 'no'.
- being unable to accept praise and compliments.
- always apologizing.
- being unable to decide what to do.
- worrying too much about upsetting others.
- feeling furious inside but unable to express these feelings to others.

vocabulary: sorry, sorry, I don't mind, don't worry about me, I hope you don't mind, er, um, excuse me

body language: clenched-handed, whining, moaning voice, downcast eyes

Assertive behaviour is:

- listening carefully to other people's point of view.
- being sensitive to other people's needs and wants.
- expressing clearly and honestly your ideas and feelings.
- asking directly for what you want.
- being honest and open with yourself as well as other people.
- not being dependent on other people's approval.
- accepting that you have rights and so do others.
- demonstrating self-respect and respect for others.
- accepting responsibility for your own actions, decisions and choices.

vocabulary: I would like, I feel, what do you think? could we discuss?

body language: direct eye contact, calm voice, relaxed posture

We are all capable of behaving aggressively, manipulatively, passively or assertively but most people have a tendency towards one form of behaviour rather than another. Work through the following questionnaires on assertiveness and discover whether there are patterns or themes in the way you deal with situations in your personal and professional life.

How Assertive are you in your Personal Relationships?

Decide how you would act in the following situations. Circle the appropriate letter. When completed find your results on page 124.

---

1. **When a friend borrows money regularly and forgets to return it,**
    Do you:

    a) get angry and refuse to listen to any excuses?

    b) drop hints about being broke?

    c) explain the effect on you and ask for it to be returned?

    d) never mention it and hope she/he remembers?

---

2. **You have planned a holiday with your partner alone. Your partner wants to invite another couple along, but you would prefer to go alone.**
    Do you:

    a) agree to go – anything to keep things on an even keel?

    b) hint that you've heard strange things about this couple and would worry about going with them?

    c) flatly refuse to go if they come?

    d) say how you feel and express your preference for going on holiday alone with your partner?

---

3. **A friend makes you feel angry and upset by her remarks about you to a mutual friend.**
    Do you:

    a) tell her that you are upset by her comments and feel let down by her?

    b) keep quiet and let it blow over?

    c) make subtle remarks about people who aren't loyal so she'll get the message?

    d) have a blazing row with her?

---

4. **Your friend/partner criticized the way you spoke to his/her mother which, in your opinion, was quite justified.**
    Do you:

    a) suggest that 'siding with mother' shows a lack of loyalty to you?
    b) say that you will speak to people exactly how you like and it is none of his/her business?
    c) apologize and say it won't happen again?
    d) let him/her know that you felt strongly about the situation and the importance of giving your opinion?

5. **Someone pushes in front of you in the cinema queue.**
    Do you:

    a) ignore them and leave it for others to comment?
    b) give the queue jumper a piece of your mind which everyone else nearby can hear?
    c) make sure you tell the queue jumper how annoyed you feel and ask him/her politely to move to the end of the queue?
    d) embarrass the queue jumper into moving by pointed comments and sarcastic remarks?

6. **Your partner makes love to you and the experience is not at all satisfactory.**
    Do you:

    a) go quiet or moody afterwards?
    b) pretend all is well and say nothing?
    c) tell your partner you aren't happy with the situation and why?
    d) start a row about selfishness or compatibility?

7. **You are aware that a waiter has taken the order of another table before yours in a restaurant noted for the slow service.**
    Do you:

    a) tell the waiter politely that the other order has been taken out of turn and express your wish for this to be changed?
    b) complain to the manager that the service is poor?
    c) ignore it and resign yourself to a longer wait?
    d) tell the waiter you have to leave/will miss your train if you are not served right away before the other table?

8. **A friend asks to borrow your mobile phone for the day but you are reluctant to lend it and want to refuse.**
    Do you:

    a) say it's out of order?
    b) point out what a cheek it is to ask you?
    c) lend it but feel resentful that you've done so?
    d) say you feel mean to refuse but you've made a decision not to lend it out to anyone?

9. **Your mother said she would stay with you for a week. Ten days have now passed and she hasn't mentioned leaving.**
    Do you:

    a) tell her you are having friends for the weekend and she'll have to leave on Friday?
    b) check with her when she's planning to leave and suggest when it would be convenient for you?
    c) keep quiet?
    d) complain that she never sticks to plans and takes your hospitality for granted?

10. **An acquaintance tells you he saw your partner having dinner in a restaurant out of town. You had been told that he/she was working at the office and feel hurt that you may have been deliberately misled.**
   Do you:

   a) decide it could have been a working dinner and choose not to mention it?

   b) question subtly about the day's activities to find out what's been happening?

   c) demand to know why you weren't told about his/her real plans for the evening?

   d) say what you've heard and explain how you feel?

11. **A member of your family criticizes your latest outfit.**
   Do you:

   a) feel upset and worry that you may have made a wrong choice?

   b) snap back at them?

   c) leave the room but make snide comments about their clothes later, or sulk?

   d) tell them you love the outfit and feel happy wearing it?

12. **Your partner leaves you waiting outside a shop for half an hour after the time you arranged to meet. This is always happening.**
   Do you:

   a) say you are cold/desperate for a drink/feeling ill?

   b) brush off the lateness as unimportant?

   c) say how annoyed you are about being kept waiting and ask him/her to be on time in future?

   d) blow your top and cause a scene?

ASSERTIVENESS IN PERSONAL RELATIONSHIPS

1.

a	b	c	d
Agg	M	Ass	P

Your result　　Agg　　M　　Ass　　P

2.

a	b	c	d
P	M	Agg	Ass

Your result　　Agg　　M　　Ass　　P

3.

a	b	c	d
Ass	P	M	Agg

Your result　　Agg　　M　　Ass　　P

4.

a	b	c	d
M	Agg	P	Ass

Your result　　Agg　　M　　Ass　　P

5.

a	b	c	d
P	Agg	Ass	M

Your result　　Agg　　M　　Ass　　P

6.

a	b	c	d
M	P	Ass	Agg

Your result　　Agg　　M　　Ass　　P

7.

a	b	c	d
Ass	Agg	P	M

Your result　　Agg　　M　　Ass　　P

8.

a	b	c	d
M	Agg	P	Ass

Your result　　Agg　　M　　Ass　　P

9.

a	b	c	d
M	Ass	P	Agg

Your result　　Agg　　M　　Ass　　P

10.	a	b	c	d		Your result	Agg	M	Ass	P
	P	M	Agg	Ass						

11.	a	b	c	d		Your result	Agg	M	Ass	P
	P	Agg	M	Ass						

12.	a	b	c	d		Your result	Agg	M	Ass	P
	M	P	Ass	Agg						

*Count up your score and read
the description which best applies
to you on the following pages.*

Total P's	_____
Total M's	_____
Total Ass's	_____
Total Agg's	_____

Mostly 'Agg's'

You may be seen as loud and forceful, as someone who stands up for herself. Often you do get your way because people are frightened of challenging you. You tend to be very competitive and so keen to score that you forget to consider the other person's point of view or acknowledge their feelings. They may feel angry, hurt or humiliated by you but you may never know this as they learn to hide their feelings from you. Sometimes you may provoke an aggressive response but you usually find one to top it! Because you like to win at everything and want to be seen as tough at all costs, you may feel the need to be constantly watchful. You may regularly feel angry, irritated, hot and bothered and unappreciated. You are losing a lot of energy in your determination to win and putting all your relationships at risk. You have learned to cope with other people by being aggressive but you can decide to change the way you react. Recognize that there is an assertive option and that these skills can be learned.

Mostly 'M's'

You are skilled at getting your own way with others and wriggling out of difficult situations but you are not direct in your approach because you are frightened of confrontation. Although you tell yourself you are protecting others it is usually a way of protecting yourself. You need to be in control and often confuse and frustrate people because they are unsure of your real feelings and intentions. Maybe you have learned to use subtle devices to get your own way and these usually work for you, but others may end up feeling used or compromised. You can also make other people feel guilty and uncomfortable if they have displeased you. Your relationships may suffer because people are never sure of the 'real you' and don't trust you with their real concerns. Superficially you may seem to approve of them, but they may detect an undercurrent of disapproval. You don't really develop the kind of close relationships you would like. You regularly feel unhappy with yourself, misunderstood, guilty and ashamed. You need to learn to be more direct and open in your relationships and let others get to know the real you!

Mostly 'P's'

You spend much of your time going along with what others want and what others *tell* you you want, for the sake of peace and quiet. Gradually you may opt out of making decisions and taking responsibility for choices in your life completely. Because other people feel forced into making decisions for you, they may feel frustrated and resentful. You hate confrontations and avoid them at all costs even if it means causing real upset to yourself. Giving in all the time may backfire on you because your 'never mind me' nature is often unappreciated and people may begin to treat you like a doormat.

You may feel hard done by and that good things happen to everyone but you. People help you up to a point but may get fed up with your negative outlook. You often put yourself down and find it difficult to acknowledge the nice things people do say about you.

You may regularly feel shy, stressed, inadequate, unhappy and guilty. You may find yourself being put last by others because you constantly put yourself last. You have learned to cope with life the best way you feel able but you need to start giving yourself more consideration, learn to know what you want and practise being more assertive.

Mostly 'Ass's'

You are confident in yourself and regularly demonstrate that you can balance your own and others' needs. You respect other people and accept your own positive and negative qualities so that you don't need to put other people down to feel comfortable with yourself. You feel in charge of yourself – your actions and your choices. If you want something from other people you don't become aggressive, demanding or whining in your request; you can ask directly for what you need. You recognize your right to be listened to, consulted and involved in decision making. If people do treat you badly or refuse your request, you don't feel let down, bitter or rejected. Your self-esteem is high and you deal with their unreasonable behaviour in an honest and direct way.

You regularly feel assured, confident and happy; well able to deal effectively with your relationships. You are likely to build up strong, close friendships because people trust you and respect your integrity. Your friends are likely to treat you in a similarly assertive way.

Some women will identify with one description, others with two and many with all four at different times! It is interesting to see if you can identify a pattern in the way you relate to others. Are you, for example, an aggressive partner and a passive daughter? Once you can recognize how you are relating then you can start to make choices and changes.

PROFESSIONAL LIFE

How Assertive are you with Work Colleagues?

Put a ✓ in the appropriate box
When completed check your score on the opposite page.

		NEVER	RARELY	SOME-TIMES	ALWAYS
1.	If I am unsure of what should be done with work I have been given, I can ask for assistance from others.				
2.	When there is an opportunity for promotion I can put myself forward.				
3.	If someone criticizes me unfairly or puts me down in front of colleagues, I can raise the topic for discussion with him/her.				
4.	I take criticism well which is deserved e.g. lateness, forgetting deadlines, etc.				
5.	I can ask for a salary increase when I think I deserve it.				
6.	If I am asked to do something at work which I feel is unfair, too difficult, outside the terms of the contract, I can say 'no' politely with excuses.				
7.	I can praise people for work well done without feeling embarrassed.				
8.	I can give criticism when it is deserved without aggression or apology.				
9.	If a work colleague is bossy or domineering I make sure I don't ignore it but deal with the situation.				
10.	I am able to make a point in a meeting in front of several work colleagues.				
11.	If someone asks me my opinion I am happy to tell them even though it's against what most people think.				
12.	If I experience sexual harassment I can tell the person calmly that I find the behaviour offensive.				
13.	I can deal easily and effectively with people in authority at work.				

How Assertive are you with Work Colleagues?
How to score

Give yourself: 5 points for 'always'
2 points for 'sometimes'
1 point for 'rarely'
0 points for 'never'

Score 50–65
You are confident and assertive in your approach to situations at work, and well able to accept positive and negative qualities in yourself and others. You can ask for what you want from others without worrying what they might say in reply. You can stand up for yourself and your opinions, express your feelings openly and honestly without being aggressive. You are prepared to accept responsibility for your own actions, decisions and choices. Keep working on assertiveness and learning more about the skills to retain this high quality of interaction with others.

Score 35–49
Although you can be assertive in many situations you tend to have 'problem' areas. It may be, for example, that you find difficulty in asserting yourself in groups or with people in authority. Try to identify those situations with which you have difficulty and, using the ideas which follow, identify the assertive skills which you need to practise to improve the way you deal with work colleagues in these situations.

Score 16–34
You are unable to be consistent in your assertive behaviour. Some days you are confident about your work, making decisions, stating your views, but the next day something goes wrong and you behave unassertively. You then worry about what other people may think, become unsure of your work and feel vulnerable to the slightest criticism. It is important that you learn to be consistent in your relationships at work, so that people know where they are with you. Choose one area to work on initially which is relatively easy to tackle and using ideas in this chapter, practise using assertive skills to effect changes in the way you relate.

Score 0–15

You find it difficult to assert yourself at work, often feeling unable to do or say what you really want. You may be afraid to assert your rights as you worry that people may see you as awkward. You worry too, that if you try to make a stand about things which concern you, you may become emotional or angry. It is important that you start to communicate more effectively. Using the information in this chapter discuss with a friend how you might start to use assertive skills to develop more fulfilling relationships at work. Practise by using role play initially and start with a relatively easy situation.

ASSESSING YOUR ASSERTIVE SKILLS

In completing the questionnaires you will have begun to think about your
assertive and non-assertive behaviour and how you respond to people in a
variety of situations. Many women feel that they are able to behave
assertively with work colleagues but find it difficult to say what they want to
with their partner or friends. Others find the opposite; they are confident and
assertive with their close friends and become tongue-tied when dealing with
people at work.

Even though satisfying relationships are vital to our well-being we seldom
take positive steps to maintain or improve them. Most of us take our
relationships for granted, allowing things to drift along, becoming fatalistic
about situations which upset us and feeling powerless to make changes.
Think about your lifestyle and answer the following questions:

Would you like to develop better working relationships?
Do you want to be more open with your family?
Do you want to become more assertive with your boss?
Do you want to develop a closer relationship with your partner?
Do you want to relate differently with groups?
Do you want to deal more confidently with strangers?

What would you like to change about the way you relate to others?

I would like to stop

I would like to start

In the next section you will be considering how to develop your assertiveness
in ways which best suit your personality. Behaving assertively may not always
get you what you want; nevertheless being assertive will help you to stay
calm and in control. The process of speaking up for yourself and expressing
your feelings will help you to feel good about yourself.

POSSIBLE AREAS OF DIFFICULTY IN DEVELOPING ASSERTIVENESS

In this section try to identify the areas where you have difficulty in behaving assertively. Use your answers to previous questionnaires and the prompts written below to help you think of your own situations.

ARE YOU ABLE TO EXPRESS YOUR POSITIVE THOUGHTS AND FEELINGS?

Examples:

In professional relationships
I like your calmness when things go wrong.
I appreciate your kindness to all the staff here.
You made an excellent contribution to the meeting today.

In personal relationships
I do appreciate what you've done for my family.
I like the way you smile at everyone.
I think you have a real flair with clothes.

ARE YOU ABLE TO EXPRESS YOUR NEGATIVE THOUGHTS AND FEELINGS?

In professional relationships
I feel upset that you didn't take my appraisal interview seriously.
I feel taken for granted when you don't acknowledge my efforts.
I feel very uncomfortable when you make racist remarks.

In personal relationships
I feel scared when you say life isn't worth living.
I resent all the time you spend working on the car.
I feel bitter about the lack of honesty in our relationship.

ARE YOU ABLE TO SAY 'NO'?

In professional relationships
No, I cannot help you with your report.
No, I cannot lend you my 'phone.
No, I won't be able to stay late tonight.

In personal relationships
No, I cannot iron your shirt.
No, I don't want to spend Christmas with your family again.
No, I don't want to help with the village hall fund.

ARE YOU ABLE TO EXPRESS YOUR ANGER?

In professional relationships
I feel mad when you're late for every meeting.
I feel really annoyed when you dismiss my contributions to the discussion.
I get angry when you come to work late without warning.

In personal relationships
I feel furious when you leave the kitchen in such a mess.
I feel cross when you can't be bothered to 'phone.
I feel angry when you behave so badly at parties.

ARE YOU ABLE TO STATE WHAT YOU BELIEVE?

In professional relationships
I think it would be better if you delegated some of your work to me.
I believe that we should ask for Peter's resignation.
I disagree with Mr Grant's ideas for the promotion.

In personal relationships
I don't agree that our financial arrangements are working well.
I think we need to ask for professional help with our sexual relationship.
I think it would be better for us all if Mum went into a nursing home.

ARE YOU ABLE TO ASK FOR WHAT YOU WANT?

In professional relationships
I would like to see the personnel officer about my progress here.
I would like to be consulted before such decisions are made in future.
I would like to be called Ms Green in future.

In personal relationships
I would like you to 'phone me more often.
I would like you to let me know by 6 p.m. if you are going to be late.
I would like us to spend more time together.

ARE YOU ABLE TO PROMOTE YOURSELF?

In professional relationships
I think I deserve a pay rise.
I feel that I am an ideal candidate for the post advertized.
I have managed several shops very successfully.

In personal relationships
I deserve a hug for keeping my temper with your sister.
I've done well sorting out our finances today.
I deserve spoiling this evening.

YOUR RIGHTS

Before you start on the practical exercises which follow, it is important to consider your basic human rights. In our relationships these may be thought of as ways in which we might reasonably expect to treat and be treated by each other.

- **I have the right to be myself.**
  Sometimes you may feel swamped by all your responsibilities but it is important to remember to make time for your own personal wants and needs.

- **I have the right to be treated as an equal.**
  On occasions where we feel less sure of ourselves we may allow ourselves to be treated as less capable or less intelligent than we are.

- **I have the right to an opinion.**
  It may be difficult to voice an opinion which is contradictory to the rest of our family's/friends'/work colleagues' views, but we have the right to express it.

- **I have the right to express my feelings.**
  It is very important to be able to identify how we feel at the time of the event and let others know how it is affecting us.

- **I have the right to make a choice.**
  It is important to feel free to make choices because we want or don't want to do something without having to justify our choice on other grounds.

- **I have the right to be wrong.**
  Many of us feel overwhelmed with anxiety when we make mistakes but it is important to recognize that we are not infallible, and that to make errors is human and natural. It may be unfortunate but it need not throw us into a turmoil of self-deceit.

- **I have the right to say 'I don't understand'.**
  Asking for an explanation when you are confused can be difficult (especially when everyone else seems to be taking things in) but you cannot know and understand everything. You are perfectly entitled to ask for clarification without feeling stupid.

- **I have the right to ask for what I want.**
  Many of us do not ask for things in a straightforward manner. We drop hints, make suggestions, hedge round the subject, hoping that someone will get the message. We feel that the request will be rejected. We worry about causing inconvenience to others or being seen as a nuisance. We must remember that we have the right to make requests of other people.

Being clear about and accepting your rights and other people's rights provides you with a good basis for assertive behaviour.

Continually consult these basic rights in your quest for more assertive relationships.

SITUATIONS IN WHICH I WOULD LIKE TO BE MORE ASSERTIVE

Bearing your rights in mind, consider 10 situations in your everyday life where you would like to behave more assertively. Think of different situations concerning work and home, family, friends, acquaintances or work colleagues. Make sure some situations are relatively easy to tackle but do include some difficult, longer term problems as well. Give each situation a score on the scale 0–10, 10 denoting very difficult situations, 1–2 indicating situations which are less difficult for you to tackle.

SITUATION: EXAMPLES	SCORE 0–10	HOW I DEAL WITH THIS NOW
Saying 'no' to my manager when he asks me to work without notice	8	Passively. I behave like a wimp and I'm too polite when he's unreasonable.
Speaking up at meetings	5	Passively. I am too quiet and worry how I'll come across.
Asking my mother to call less often	9	Manipulatively. I pretend I'm going away. I don't answer the 'phone on Fridays.
Asking my partner to help without nagging	2	Aggressively. I lose my cool.
Asking people not to smoke in my car	3	Manipulatively. I cough and say I'm worried I'll get asthma.

SITUATIONS IN WHICH I WOULD LIKE TO BE MORE ASSERTIVE

SITUATION	SCORE 0–10	HOW I DEAL WITH THIS NOW
1.		
2.		
3.		
4.		
5.		
6.		
7.		
8.		
9.		
10.		

COMMUNICATING ASSERTIVELY

There are five important steps in using an assertive approach.

> **1. NAME THE PERSON AND IDENTIFY EXACTLY WHAT THE PROBLEM IS.**

Be careful that you keep to one issue which focuses on the behaviour rather than labelling the person. For example say, 'John, when you stay in bed all morning ...' rather than 'John, you are lazy'.

Keep the statement short and to the point.

> **2. SAY WHAT YOU THINK AND FEEL, CLEARLY, DIRECTLY AND WITH CONVICTION.**

Take responsibility for your feelings. Be clear that it is the **behaviour** of the person which has given rise to your anger, irritation or worry. For example say, 'I feel irritated when you read the paper when we are eating', rather than, 'you make me irritated'.

> **3. SAY SPECIFICALLY WHAT YOU WANT TO HAPPEN.**

Be very clear **exactly** what you want. Asking for a small reasonable change is much more likely to be successful than dropping hints, whining or becoming aggressive. This behaviour may exacerbate the situation.

> **4. ASK HOW THE OTHER PERSON FEELS ABOUT YOUR REQUEST AND LISTEN TO THE RESPONSE.**

Being assertive includes understanding the other person's point of view. You need to listen attentively and demonstrate by the way you listen and respond, that you are interested in, and want to understand their view of the situation. Listening well to others takes special effort, particularly when you have strong feelings about their behaviour. Listening to others attentively doesn't mean you agree with them, but it demonstrates understanding which helps keep communication going.

---

5.   LOOK FOR A JOINT SOLUTION.

Try to work out a reasonable compromise right away rather than leaving things unresolved. Make sure you are both satisfied with the decision made.

Being assertive does not always come easily or naturally to most women. Becoming relaxed and confident in using assertive skills takes time and effort. Start with the least sensitive situations first and practise being assertive on your own or with a friend. Role playing offers the most effective way of helping you to develop the skills. Work together using the five steps. Make sure you give feedback to each other.

ASSERTIVENESS IN PERSONAL RELATIONSHIPS

Choose one situation in your personal relationship with a partner, friend or member of your family where you would like to behave more assertively. Using the example as a guide, fill in the questionnaire which follows.

---

1. NAME THE PERSON AND IDENTIFY EXACTLY WHAT THE PROBLEM IS.

Example   **Your Situation**
Jan, when you leave all your washing-up
until the next morning ...

---

2. SAY WHAT YOU THINK AND FEEL, CLEARLY, DIRECTLY AND WITH CONVICTION.

Example   **Your Situation**
I feel irritated because I have to eat
breakfast surrounded by dirty crockery.

---

3. SAY SPECIFICALLY WHAT YOU WANT TO HAPPEN.

Example   **Your Situation**
I would really appreciate your washing-up
after your meal.

---

4. ASK HOW THE OTHER PERSON FEELS ABOUT YOUR REQUEST AND LISTEN TO THE RESPONSE.

Example   **Your Situation**
How do you feel about this?

Her Reply: I'm too tired in the evenings.
It's my flat as well as yours you know!

5. LOOK FOR A JOINT SOLUTION.

Example

I know how tired you are in the evenings. But I would like to have breakfast without clearing your dishes away first. Could we think of a solution that would suit both of us?

Her Reply: I don't mind stacking it in a pile by the sink.

That suits me if the table is cleared.

Your Situation

ASSERTIVENESS IN PROFESSIONAL RELATIONSHIPS

Choose one situation with a work colleague where you would like to behave more assertively. Using the example as a guide, fill in the questionnaire which follows.

---

1. NAME THE PERSON AND IDENTIFY EXACTLY WHAT THE PROBLEM IS.

Example   **Your Situation**
John, when you expect me to work late
without any warning ...

---

2. SAY WHAT YOU THINK AND FEEL, CLEARLY, DIRECTLY AND WITH CONVICTION.

Example   **Your Situation**
I feel upset because I often have to cancel
other arrangements at the last minute.

---

3. SAY SPECIFICALLY WHAT YOU WANT TO HAPPEN.

Example   **Your Situation**
I would appreciate very much your letting
me know earlier in the day if I'm needed.

---

4. ASK HOW THE OTHER PERSON FEELS ABOUT YOUR REQUEST AND LISTEN TO THE RESPONSE.

Example   **Your Situation**
Do you feel this would be possible?

His Reply: You should be prepared to
work late at the drop of a hat if you want
to get on.

---

5.   LOOK FOR A JOINT SOLUTION

Example

I do want to get on and I am very happy
to help if I have the request earlier.
Would that be possible?

His Reply: Would lunch time be early
enough?

Yes, that would give me plenty of time to
rearrange things. Thank you for agreeing
to that.

Your Situation

ASSERTIVENESS IN PRACTICE

Write down an assertive approach to the following situations.

A friend has volunteered your help to organize a charity run in the village. Your time is already committed and you are furious that she/he assumed that you would help, without checking with you first.

Write down what you would say:

You have come home from work expecting your partner to have prepared your meal as agreed. You find the house in a mess and no food in sight.

Write down what you would say:

A colleague has written to your boss complaining about your time-keeping. You are very upset about this.

Write down what you would say:

Your mother has volunteered to help look after your partner and child while you are in hospital having a baby. Your partner is adamant that he doesn't want her to stay and you would prefer that she didn't . You want to decline her help.

Write down what you would say:

RESPONDING TO OTHERS ASSERTIVELY

In the exercises you have completed so far, you have been practising using assertive skills in situations where **you** initiated the action. On many occasions you are required to **respond** to the action of other people, for example, when they become angry or aggressive, when they request something of you, when they praise or blame you or ask your opinion.

These situations may pose more problems for you because you are put on the spot and forced to reply without having had time to prepare yourself.

Dealing with Anger and Aggression from Others

Consider the following situations and tick the statement which most closely describes your likely behaviour.

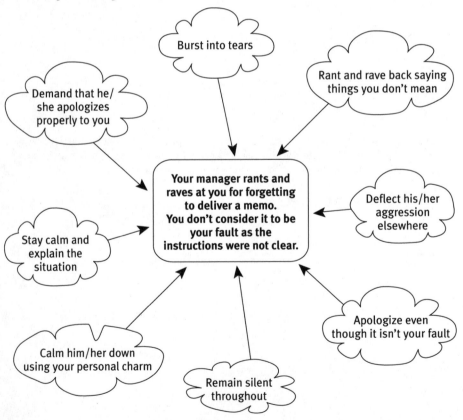

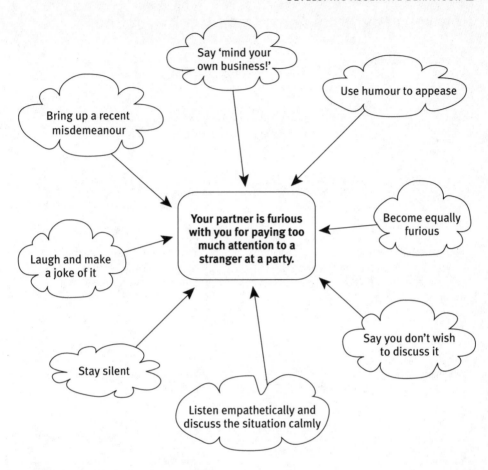

Is there a difference in the way you react to aggression at home and at work? Do you behave aggressively with family and passively with work colleagues or vice versa?

Many women find difficulty in coping with anger and aggression from others. Verbal attacks can leave you feeling exhausted, hurt or humiliated. The scene may stay with you for days, weeks or even years. You may spend a disproportionate amount of time discussing the incident with friends and colleagues, or going over it in your own mind, reliving the experience and reliving the feelings of anger, frustration, fear or bitterness. Consider how anger and aggression from others may affect your feelings and behaviour. We will use the examples referred to earlier in this section.

How your Partner's Aggression may Affect You

Statement (partner)

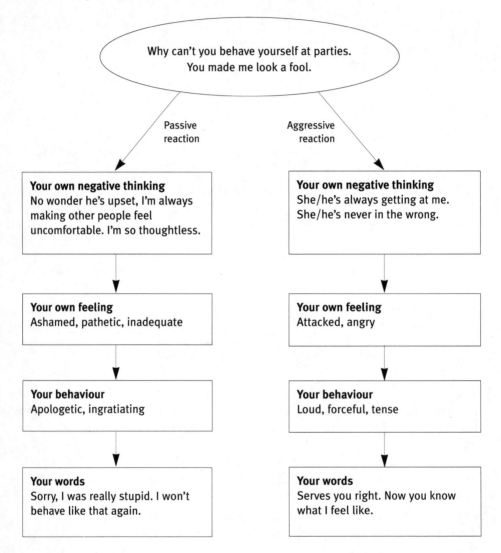

Why can't you behave yourself at parties.
You made me look a fool.

Passive reaction

Aggressive reaction

Your own negative thinking
No wonder he's upset, I'm always making other people feel uncomfortable. I'm so thoughtless.

Your own negative thinking
She/he's always getting at me. She/he's never in the wrong.

Your own feeling
Ashamed, pathetic, inadequate

Your own feeling
Attacked, angry

Your behaviour
Apologetic, ingratiating

Your behaviour
Loud, forceful, tense

Your words
Sorry, I was really stupid. I won't behave like that again.

Your words
Serves you right. Now you know what I feel like.

HOW YOUR MANAGER'S AGGRESSION MAY AFFECT YOU

Statement (aggressive manager)

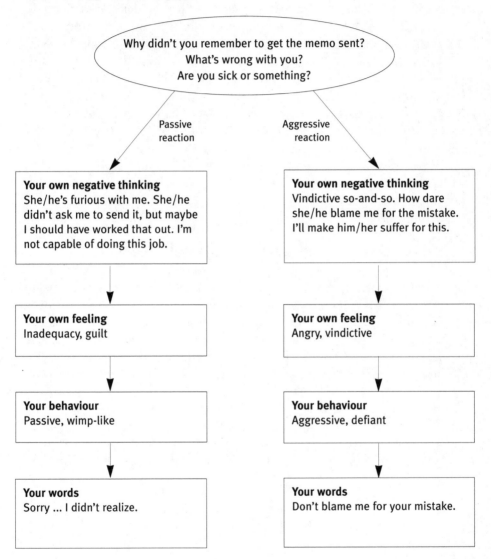

Why didn't you remember to get the memo sent?
What's wrong with you?
Are you sick or something?

Passive
reaction

Aggressive
reaction

Your own negative thinking
She/he's furious with me. She/he
didn't ask me to send it, but maybe
I should have worked that out. I'm
not capable of doing this job.

Your own negative thinking
Vindictive so-and-so. How dare
she/he blame me for the mistake.
I'll make him/her suffer for this.

Your own feeling
Inadequacy, guilt

Your own feeling
Angry, vindictive

Your behaviour
Passive, wimp-like

Your behaviour
Aggressive, defiant

Your words
Sorry ... I didn't realize.

Your words
Don't blame me for your mistake.

USING ASSERTIVENESS POSITIVELY

Although you cannot prevent other people from behaving aggressively you can control your own reaction and minimize the psychological impact. Learning to respond assertively to aggression will help you to retain control of your own behaviour. Relationships at work are often different from those in your private life because of inequality in terms of power, authority, the issues of money and job security and the complexity of coping with colleagues on both a personal and professional level. However, do remember not to take anger personally. Some colleagues may be angry as a result of frustration about another situation; the anger is not intentionally aimed at you. Other people may be aggressive towards you because this way of behaving makes them feel powerful and in control, whereas, in reality, they are feeling incompetent and insecure. If you are aware that bad temper and rudeness is one way of protecting a fragile self-esteem then you may feel more confident in asserting yourself.

In personal relationships you may feel less inhibited in expressing your feelings. In response to aggressive behaviour from your partner, friend or a member of your family, you may ask why not attack back?, why bother with his/her feelings? If you do respond aggressively, you are likely to be out of control and irrational rather than responding from a position of power and control. Unfortunately, aggression frequently elicits counter-aggression and a no-win situation for everyone. The aggressive outburst often results in guilt and annoyance with yourself.

Behaving passively in response to aggression may seem to be the safest alternative. Unfortunately this way of behaving, avoiding confrontation and hiding feelings, may become a habit which eventually leads to a total breakdown of communication in expressing feelings and emotions.

HANDLING AGGRESSIVE BEHAVIOUR

Describe a recent experience in your personal or professional life when you dealt ineffectively with someone's aggressive behaviour towards you.

DESCRIBE THE SITUATION	YOUR SITUATION
Example I was working with a colleague making a transparency when I made a mistake and the machine jammed.	
Describe how the other person behaved and what he/she said. He lost his temper and started swearing at me.	**Describe how the other person behaved and what he/she said.**
Describe how you felt. I felt angry and afraid that someone could be so unreasonable.	**Describe how you felt.**
Describe your behaviour. I burst into tears and left the room.	**Describe your behaviour.**
Describe what you said. I didn't mean to ... I'm sorry	**Describe what you said.**
What were the consequences? The atmosphere between us remains tense. We only speak when it's essential. I feel worried that he might behave like this again with me.	**What were the consequences?**

RESPONDING ASSERTIVELY TO ANGER AND AGGRESSION FROM OTHERS

Aggression is the most difficult emotion to cope with for many women. The temptation to fight or flight is strong. Your main aim must be to stem the flow of anger in yourself and the other person; to get the interaction on the assertive level so that you can both deal with the issues calmly and feel comfortable about your discussion later. In order to do this you must take steps to remain calm yourself, and acknowledge the other person's feelings. This will help to diffuse the emotion.

---

1. Take a deep breath.

Use relaxation techniques.

Use positive selftalk e.g. 'I can stay in control. I have dealt well with these situations before.'

Do not say anything out loud.

---

2. Listen carefully.

Maintain eye contact but do not smile.

Ensure your body language conveys your calm, confident manner.

---

3. Make sure you are clear what the other person is saying and why they are saying it.

Ask questions for information and clarification.

Keep your voice assertive and demonstrate that you are aware of their negative feelings.

I can see you are very annoyed about this.

4. Say where you stand and how you feel.

I see things differently from you ...'

I have spent time working on this too, and I feel annoyed that ...

5. If the aggression continues, restate your position keeping your statement short, firm and basic.

Make sure you take account of new information received.

I understand that John's behaviour has made things worse. However, I cannot agree with you that ...

Indicate your negative feelings. *I feel angry that you are still talking so loud.*

6. If the aggression continues, indicate what the consequences will be.

Use a calm, matter-of-fact tone.

Ann, if you continue to make these accusations without listening to me, I will put the phone down.

John, if you cannot discuss this without shouting, I suggest we arrange another time to meet.

USING ASSERTIVENESS WHEN YOU WANT TO SAY 'NO'

Many women find it difficult to say 'no' directly and clearly. They worry about being selfish, rude or small-minded and become concerned that other people may feel hurt, let down or behave aggressively towards them. In fact the opposite is often true. People feel embarrassed or uncomfortable when they are subjected to excuses, explanations or guilty expressions which could have been avoided by a plain, straightforward 'no'. Remember that other people have the right to ask, but you have the right to say 'no'. When you say 'no' you are refusing the request, not rejecting the person. Consider some of the pitfalls of saying 'yes' when you want to say 'no'.

• You may find yourself spending hours extricating yourself from unwanted commitments and concocting all sorts of acceptable excuses.

• You may take on too much and find life and work stressful. In submerging your own needs, you may actually end up achieving far less for others because you are physically and mentally exhausted.

• You may feel resentful or angry about becoming involved with something you wanted to refuse. You are unlikely to feel committed to, or interested in, the task undertaken and may dampen other's enthusiasm.

• You may have negative feelings about yourself for failing to refuse the request – feelings of inadequacy and low self-esteem.

REFUSING REQUESTS IN YOUR PERSONAL AND PROFESSIONAL LIFE

Consider the type of request, the people, and the circumstances when you find refusal difficult. Tick statements which apply to you. Add your own statements where appropriate.

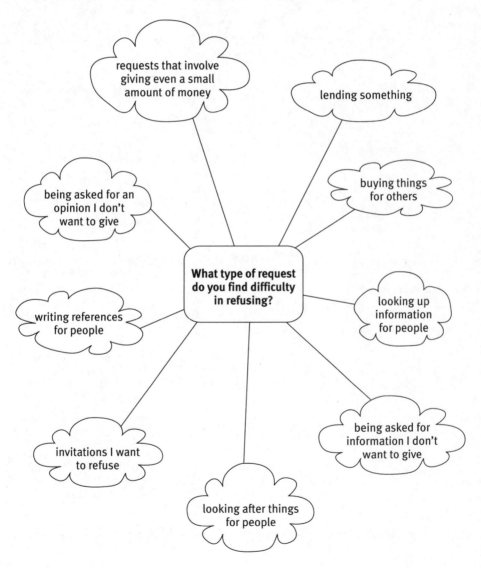

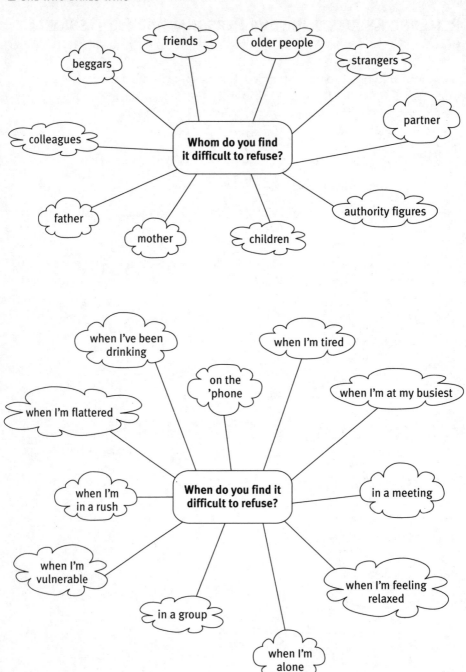

SAYING 'NO' IN PERSONAL RELATIONSHIPS

Choose a situation in your personal life when you said 'yes' when you would have preferred to say 'no'.

DISCUSS THE SITUATION	YOUR SITUATION AND THE REQUEST
Example My partner wanted me to visit his family at Christmas rather than mine.	
How I felt about the situation I didn't want to go because we spend Easter and New Year there every year.	**How I felt about the situation**
Why I said 'yes' He is closer to his family than I am to mine. He finds my father boring and makes the stay worrying for me.	**Why I said 'yes'**
What I would have liked to say No, we spend most holidays with your family and I would prefer to visit mine this Christmas.	**What I would have liked to say**

SAYING 'NO' IN PROFESSIONAL RELATIONSHIPS

Choose a situation in your professional life when you said 'yes' when you would have preferred to say 'no'.

DISCUSS THE SITUATION	YOUR SITUATION AND THE REQUEST
Example I was asked to work late when I had arranged to meet a friend in town after work.	
How I felt about the situation I felt angry that I'd been asked to work late without warning. I felt taken for granted since any arrangements I'd made weren't considered important.	**How I felt about the situation**
Why I said 'yes' I was afraid that I would jeopardize my chances of promotion if I refused.	**Why I said 'yes'**
What I would have liked to say No, I won't be able to work late tonight; I have made other arrangements which cannot be changed.	**What I would have liked to say**

USING ASSERTIVENESS WHEN YOU WANT TO SAY 'NO'

---

1. NOTE YOUR IMMEDIATE REACTION AND TRUST IT.

Your body will give you a warning about how you want to respond. Your shoulders, legs and mouth in particular, will give you an indication of how you feel.

---

2. GIVE YOURSELF TIME.

Do not answer before you think. Ask for more information, or time to think about it.

---

3. SAY 'NO' AT THE BEGINNING OF THE STATEMENT WITHOUT APOLOGIZING OR MAKING EXCUSES.

Keep your statement short and true. '*No I cannot baby-sit on Thursday*' is far preferable to '*well I'm not really sure. My mother said she was coming on Thursday and anyway it's an awkward day for Mike. I'm terribly sorry, but ...*'. If you invent an excuse it makes you feel guilty and it is often recognized as such by the other person. People want to know where they stand and a clear 'no' makes everyone's life easier. If you feel that you will spare other's feelings by saying 'yes' initially and then letting them down gradually, consider whose feelings you are protecting. How do you feel when someone doesn't turn up who said 'yes' initially, or lets you down at the last minute with a 'headache'?

---

4. DO NOT HOVER AROUND AFTER YOU HAVE SAID 'NO'.

You may confuse the situation and encourage the other person to change your mind. Leave the room, or put the phone down when you have made the decision to say 'no'.

---

5. ACKNOWLEDGE YOUR FEELINGS AND THEIRS.

Do make a simple statement which expresses truly how you feel.

I feel very guilty for not offering to help at the bazaar.

I feel ungrateful having to refuse when you've baby-sat for me so often.

I find it difficult to have to say 'no' to helping you write the report for tomorrow.

---

6. ASK HOW THEY FEEL AND OFFER AN ALTERNATIVE WHERE POSSIBLE.

There are bound to be situations where people feel let down or rejected by your refusal. By asking how they feel, you can give the other person space to express their feelings and help them recognize that their needs have not been ignored. By offering alternatives, where possible, you demonstrate a real desire to offer help.

You may feel guilty for refusing requests assertively at first. However, it will get easier with practice. The benefits from being able to say 'no' clearly, directly and honestly include:

- Having more time to spend on things you want to say 'yes' to.
- People trusting you to say what you mean.
- Feeling happier and more confident about making decisions.
- Having more self-respect.
- Developing more open and honest relationships personally and professionally.

GIVING AND RECEIVING POSITIVE AND APPRECIATIVE COMMENTS

Giving and receiving praise and appreciation is an important aspect of assertiveness. However, the art of giving compliments in a sincere, assertive manner, and receiving them without embarrassment or awkwardness is a difficult task for many women in our culture, where many people may regard compliments with suspicion. Sometimes these worries are based on previous experiences of giving praise which have been unrewarding. For example, you may have praised someone's hairstyle only to receive the reply, 'I haven't even washed it, it looks awful.' Your praising of someone's effort at work may have met with a sarcastic reply. 'Oh I'm glad somebody's noticed.' In work situations, people in positions of authority often become concerned that they may be seen as 'soft' or a 'pushover'. If they praise others, they may mistakenly believe that praising people will curtail effort and serves no useful purpose. In fact the opposite is true; people benefit tremendously from receiving positive and appreciative comments, although their defensive or embarrassed reactions may suggest otherwise. With positive feedback friends and colleagues are more likely to feel positive about themselves, to be co-operative, to feel appreciated, and consequently put far more effort into their work and relationships. Sadly, all too often we forget to tell others how we feel, thank them for things they have done, and show our appreciation for their concern or loyalty.

GIVING AND RECEIVING POSITIVE AND APPRECIATIVE COMMENTS

Choose a situation in your professional life when you wish you had said something appreciative, but didn't.

PROFESSIONAL LIFE	YOUR SITUATION
Example Situation My manager went out of her way to make sure I was given a pay rise.	
What I said *I really needed the extra money – thanks*	**What I said**
Why I said this I couldn't think of an appropriate remark. I was afraid that if I thanked her more personally I would be seen as 'crawling'.	**Why I said this**
Consequences I worry that she thinks I don't appreciate her effort.	**Consequences**
What I would like to say *I value the time and trouble you took to secure my pay rise. I really appreciate your effort. Thank you very much.*	**What I would like to say**
Benefits She would feel appreciated and more likely to do the same for other people. I would be much happier with my behaviour.	**Benefits**

GIVING AND RECEIVING POSITIVE AND APPRECIATIVE COMMENTS

Choose a situation in your personal life when you wish you had said something appreciative, but didn't.

PERSONAL LIFE	YOUR SITUATION
Example Situation My partner looked after the children for the weekend while I went to visit a friend.	
What I said *Oh you managed to cope. I expect you are more tired than you anticipated.*	**What I said**
Why I said this He is always dismissing my tiredness as lack of organization.	**Why I said this**
Consequences He spent all evening telling me how he organized the weekend.	**Consequences**
What I would like to say *Thank you for looking after the children so well. I really appreciated the time I spent alone with Anne.*	**What I would like to say**
Benefits We would both feel appreciated. He would feel positive about the weekend, and likely to be willing to repeat the task.	**Benefits**

GIVING POSITIVE AND APPRECIATIVE COMMENTS ASSERTIVELY

If you want to say something appreciative it is essential to do so assertively to avoid any misunderstanding. You do not want the receiver to wonder 'what is she after?' 'I don't believe that', 'what does she **really** mean?' These reactions usually arise in response to praise offered passively, accompanied by embarrassment, whispered almost inaudibly, or given in a gushing manner with a false smile or manner.

Practise giving compliments assertively using the guidelines below.

> **1. LOOK DIRECTLY AT THE OTHER PERSON WITHOUT STARING. SMILE. MAINTAIN A RELAXED BODY POSTURE.**

> **2. KEEP THE MESSAGE SHORT AND TO THE POINT.**

I like your shoes – they really suit you.
Thank you for being so prompt today; it really helped.

Often we disguise our meaning because we are hesitant, apologetic, or our comments are too flowery or generalized. This following comment is meant to be appreciative, but could convey the opposite meaning:

I do hope you don' t mind my commenting; I know I'm one for making sure things are organized well, but you did very well today.

> **3. USE 'I' STATEMENTS AND INCLUDE THE OTHER PERSON'S NAME.**

I admire you, Dave, for ...
Anne, I like the way you ...
I valued your contribution to the meeting Paul.

> **4. MAKE THE STATEMENT SPECIFIC.**

I liked the way you read the report today, rather than *you did well today.*
I loved the way you decorated the bathroom, rather than *the house looks nice.*
Try to avoid generalizations such as *it was good, it all went well.*

Specific feedback is more likely to raise self-awareness in the other person and encourage confidence in the repetition of their performance.

RESPONDING TO POSITIVE AND APPRECIATIVE COMMENTS FROM OTHERS

All too often you may feel uncomfortable and embarrassed, or behave defensively when you are on the receiving end of praise. You may have come to believe that it is impolite to accept the compliment, or feel that it is putting you under some sort of obligation.

All too often you may find yourself making a dismissive comment.

Thanks for making the cake.
Your Reply   *Oh it was nothing – it didn't take me a minute.*

You may find yourself denying the compliment in the following way:

You made a good presentation this morning.
Your Reply   *Not really, I didn't do it half as well as Mary does.*

You may cover your embarrassment by returning the compliment to the other person immediately.

I think your garden looks delightful.
Your Reply   *Oh yours is just as nice.*

Occasionally you may return an aggressive comment.

Your review of the article was excellent.
Your Reply   *You thought it excellent? I thought it was a load of rubbish.*

Both the passive and aggressive responses have the effect of putting the other person down and reducing the chance that they will give compliments next time.

RECEIVING POSITIVE AND APPRECIATIVE COMMENTS ASSERTIVELY

---

1. THANK THE GIVER. USE THE PERSON'S NAME. MAINTAIN EYE CONTACT. SMILE.

Thank you, Bruce.

---

2. KEEP THE RESPONSE SHORT.

I'm so glad you think so.

---

3. ACCEPT THE PRAISE IF YOU AGREE WITH IT.

Thanks, I was pleased with the way the meeting went as well.

---

4. IF YOU DISAGREE WITH THE PRAISE, STILL THANK THE GIVER BUT QUALIFY YOUR REPLY.

Thanks for saying so, Jane, but I honestly felt I could have done better.
I'm glad you think it suits me, but I don't feel so sure.

Handling Criticism in your Personal and Professional Relationships

Most of us are extremely vulnerable to any form of criticism directed towards us. Our memories of critical comments and disapproving looks from our childhood experiences and past relationships can have such a powerful effect on us today that we will do anything to avoid criticism and disapproval in our everyday lives. The memories of being labelled stupid, a wimp, a tell-tale tit or criticized for being ungrateful, sloppy or bad at maths are often as painful as they were 20, 30 or 40 years ago. When we are criticized as adults we invariably end up feeling exactly as we did as children; hurt, angry or neglected. We have learnt to mistrust people who criticize us and immediately perceive them as overpowering or untrustworthy. We fail to recognize that the criticism is usually directed at an aspect of our behaviour and not our total personality. We seldom use the criticism constructively or benefit in any way from the experience. The fear of criticism has such a powerful effect on our behaviour that it may well determine how we present ourselves, how we relate to people, the career we choose and the way we live. However, although it does take courage to listen assertively to critical comments from others, it can be beneficial. You may learn how others see you, and the effect you have on them. This knowledge may enable you to decide whether or not to change your behaviour.

Choose a Recent Experience in your Personal Life when you Handled Criticism Passively or Aggressively.

EXAMPLE SITUATION	YOUR SITUATION
I forgot to buy my mother's vegetables on my way back from work.	
What was said to you? *You have a memory like a sieve.*	**What was said to you?**
Was it true? I do forget things sometimes, but I have never forgotten her shopping before.	**Was it true?**
How did you feel? Furious.	**How did you feel?**
What did you say? *Sorry, I had a lot on my mind today.*	**What did you say?**
What was the response? *You'll have to get organized.*	**What was the response?**
What happened? I sulked.	**What happened?**
Did anything change as a result? No.	**Did anything change as a result?**

Choose a Situation in your Professional Life where you Handled Criticism Passively or Aggressively.

EXAMPLE SITUATION	YOUR SITUATION
I was criticized by the porter for leaving the door of the car park unlocked at 7 p.m. He informed my manager that I was the last to leave and I had forgotten to lock up.	
What was said? *You left the door unlocked last night. I've reported you because it's happened before!*	**What was said?**
Was it true? No. There were two other cars in the car park when I left.	**Was it true?**
How did you feel? I was angry as the porter should have checked his facts before accusing me.	**How did you feel?**
What did you say? *Why can't you get your facts right before accusing people?*	**What did you say?**
What was the response? *You young ones are far too cocky – think you know it all.*	**What was the response?**
What happened? The row escalated.	**What happened?**
Did anything change as a result? The relationship got worse. He is now desperate for me to make a mistake.	**Did anything change as a result?**

RECEIVING CRITICISM ASSERTIVELY

---

1. LISTEN CAREFULLY TO THE CRITICISM KEEPING A SOUND INNER DIALOGUE.

I may have made a mistake but it isn't a disaster.
Everyone makes mistakes at some time – I'm no different.
This is an unfair comment, but I will keep calm and deal with it professionally.

---

2. CLARIFY THE CRITICISM.

Be sure that you know exactly what the criticism is or why it is being given.
Could you give me some examples of this?
Can you tell me exactly when this occurred?
Who exactly has complained about my attendance?

---

3. DISTINGUISH BETWEEN TRUE, PARTLY TRUE AND TOTALLY FALSE.

If it is true:

1.	Acknowledge the truth.	*Yes, I am untidy.*
2.	Explain how you feel.	*I am really sorry I left the room in a mess.*
3.	Try to empathize.	*I realize it gets you down.*
4.	Offer a solution if you want to.	*I'll tidy things up this evening.*

If it is partly true:

1.	Agree with the bit that is partly true.	*Yes, I forgot to post the letters.*
2.	Make it clear the rest is untrue.	However, I have never forgotten to deal with the post before.
3.	Say how you feel	I feel disappointed that you think this happens often.

If it was totally false:

1.	Reject the criticism. Use 'I' statements.	I don't accept the blame for that. On the contrary, I have never refused to meet your work colleagues socially.
2.	Add your positive thoughts.	I am always very friendly towards them.
3.	Ask for clarification.	Could you tell me why you think I'm being unsociable?

Use the criticism to your advantage:

1. Receive it with an open mind.
2. Learn from the feedback. Are you able to see more clearly how you appear to others? Can you gain insights into how your behaviour affects them?
3. Decide to change if that would work and benefit others.
4. Think about it, deal with it, learn from it, then forget about it.

RESPONDING ASSERTIVELY TO CRITICISM

Refer back to the situations of received criticism in your personal and
professional relationships on pages 168 and 169. Write down an assertive
response you might have given to the criticism.

PERSONAL LIFE

Describe the situation and what was said
Your assertive response
What might have been the reaction and response?
What might have happened as a result?

PROFESSIONAL LIFE

Describe the situation and what was said
Your assertive response
What might have been the reaction and response?
What might have happened as a result?

SUMMARY AND ACTION

In this section you have clarified what you mean by assertiveness, identified the themes and patterns in the way you deal with other people and worked through examples of how to be assertive in several different situations.

Write down some situations in which you are going to practise being more assertive.

Action

What action do you need to take now to develop your assertive skills further?

- Do you need to join an assertiveness group? Check local papers and publications for what's on – night school and day school classes are usually available.
- Do you want to read about assertiveness in greater depth? Books recommended include: *A Woman in Your Own Right*, Anne Dickson – Quartet (1982). *The Positive Woman*, Gael Lindenfield – Thorsons (1992).
- Tackle some of the easier situations you have written down. Engage the help of a friend to role play and help you to practise.
- Keep believing in yourself. Your ability to do so will determine your future success.
- Keep notes on your progess so that you can learn from your experience.

SITUATION	WHAT HAPPENED	HOW I FELT	WHAT I NEED TO DO NEXT TIME

Part four

DEVELOPING MANAGEMENT SKILLS

Being more assertive in your relationships with others will have helped you to recognize the value of being clear about what you want and of planning what you are going to say for effective communication. You can gradually build on these basic assertive skills to develop a more structured approach in dealing with other changes you may want to make in your life. Life for many women is complex, with many options to think about and choices to make. You may be juggling several jobs at the same time and feel nothing is ever done to your satisfaction. Developing good management skills must become a top priority for you in working towards your personal and professional fulfilment.

WHAT ARE MANAGEMENT SKILLS?

Management skills are to do with planning and organizing, achieving goals, making things happen and gaining control over what happens to you both personally and professionally. Management skills are not reserved for those in high-powered executive positions; everyone can benefit from their use. Managing your life is also about gaining satisfaction from the tasks, realizing your potential and enjoying life to the full. The last point is most important. It is no use being organized and efficient if you are not getting out of life what you want and, so far as is possible, doing things the way **you** want to do them. You may be spending so much time dealing with other people's lives that you are neglecting your own needs. Many people mistakenly assume that spontaneity disappears when they develop good management skills. Nothing is further from the truth. Management skills will help you to become more open and flexible, prepared to meet challenges and to make the most of opportunities offered.

Management skills include:

- being clear about where you are, where you want to go and being aware of the choices open to you.
- being able to motivate other people to aid you – friends, family or colleagues.
- being able to choose options wisely.
- being able to prioritize.
- being able to plan time, to organize yourself and others.
- being able to delegate to others efficiently.
- being flexible in your approach so that you can adapt easily to changing circumstances.

Assess your current management skills by completing the questionnaire which follows.

How Good are Your Management Skills?

Put a ✓ in the appropriate column.
Turn to next page to check your score.

Do you . . .

	NEVER	SOME-TIMES	OFTEN	ALWAYS
1. Write a list of things that must be done today?				
2. Refuse to take work home at weekends or in the evening on a regular basis?				
3. Say 'no' to unscheduled interruptions?				
4. Delegate easily and efficiently?				
5. Put tasks in order of priority and work on them in that order?				
6. Meet deadlines without any real hassle, e.g. without having to stay up half the night?				
7. Arrive on time for appointments?				
8. Plan time to give feedback and information to people who work for you on a regular basis?				
9. Think about where you want to be in your career in 5 years' time?				
10. Change ideas/plans easily when difficulties arise?				
11. Remember other people's birthdays/ anniversaries etc?				
12. Shop systematically i.e. once a month, once a week?				
13. Take regular exercise?				
14. Have your car regularly serviced?				
15. Keep an up-to-date, well ordered file of personal affairs, bank statements, insurance etc?				
16. Watch only those T.V. programmes you've planned to watch?				
17. Have a place for everything so that you don't spend time looking for things?				
18. Have a system for knowing when stocks run low so that you don't run out of stamps, salt, loo roll, etc?				
19. Enjoy leisure time with partner, family without feeling preoccupied?				
20. Have social events planned well ahead in your diary that **you** have organized?				

How Good are Your Management Skills?
Results of Questionnaire.

Score: Always   5
           Often   3
           Sometimes   1
           Never   0

Your total score

80–100   You have excellent management skills which you apply well at home and at work. Your clear thinking, efficiency and ability to plan ahead mean that you make the most of your present job and gain real satisfaction from your social life. However, you have the drive, energy and determination to meet ever greater challenges.

55–79   Your management skills are good and you generally have a clear view of where you are and what you want to do. Occasionally your plans go wrong and things don't work as well as you expected, but these hiccups are rare. You are likely to enjoy a management role. Are you realizing your potential in your career?

26–54   Sometimes you sail through the day and everything goes to plan. At other times you find you've mislaid something important, forgotten to cancel an order, put off 'phoning someone 'until tomorrow'. It is important to have an overview of your life at home and at work and to focus on the problematic areas. You could find yourself with more time and energy to do what you most enjoy.

0–25   You find managing your private and professional life a real chore at times. You swing from feeling angry and depressed about things to being resigned to a life that often seems chaotic. You can learn management skills. Start by dealing with one thing that you've been putting off for ages – for example clearing your desk top of unnecessary clutter, or writing a letter to the insurance company. Take one step at a time and you'll gradually feel less hassled.

The first ten questions on the questionnaire are concerned with your management skills at work; the remaining questions with your management skills at home. It may be useful to see if your management skills are stronger in one area than another. Could you transfer some of the management strategies you use at work to your home life and vice versa?

MANAGING YOUR TIME

Time management is about knowing what you want and need to do, setting clear priorities for yourself and making sure you achieve them. Although time management is usually associated with work, you will gain real benefits in your personal, social and family life as well by using your time more effectively. A more organized lifestyle means extra hours to spend and more energy to use. Practical techniques are important, although learning about yourself, your feelings, attitude, beliefs and values must come first. Unless you are clear about these personal issues, time management strategies will not work half as well for you.

Time management is about finding ways to enjoy life to the full. It is very much concerned with doing things you **want** to do as well as things you must do; doing things you want to do **today** as well as in the future.

Ask yourself some general questions about your use of time.

- What part of my life am I enjoying most?
- What satisfaction am I getting from the time and energy I am expending?
- What would I like to do that I don't have time for?
- What would I like to change about my use of time?
- What do I want to spend more time doing at work?
- What do I want to spend more time doing at home?

Weekly and Daily Time Log Activity

In order to make a start on managing your time you need to be aware of what you actually do with your time at present. This knowledge is an essential first step to change; it gives you a basic idea of what you do, how long things take, how you deal with interruptions, how long you spend on the 'phone, etc. Over the next week make a detailed record of how you spend your time in your personal and professional life. There are two charts to complete. A Weekly Time Log in which you write down your general activities over one week. You may record how you have used your time at the end of each day but twice or three times a day is preferable. On two days during the week complete a more detailed record of your activities on the Daily Time Log. Invent your own shorthand and symbols to make keeping the chart easier. You will need to fill in the daily time log very regularly, noting the time you start or change tasks rather than doing this retrospectively. It is important to fill in everything you do, social chats, coffee breaks, interruptions – everything. Some people find more difficulty than others in keeping a time log as they are on the move or in situations where writing is impossible. However, there are usually ways round the problem with a little imagination.

WEEKLY TIME LOG

		Mon	Tues	Wed	Thurs	Fri	Sat	Sun
	10-12							
	8-10							
	6-8							
	4-6							
p.m.	2-4							
	12-2							
	10-12							
	8-10							
a.m.	6-8							
	4-6							
	2-4							
	12-2							

DAILY TIME LOG

TIME	ACTIVITY	TIME SPENT

WEEKLY ACTIVITY CHART

When you have completed the chart you will be able to analyze exactly how your time was spent. Fill in the 'activity chart' below so that you can see more clearly which activities took up major portions of your time. Try to estimate, in one week, how long you spent on each activity. A few common activities are listed as a start.

ACTIVITY	HOURS SPENT
Sleeping	
Travelling	
Eating	
Shopping	
Household tasks	
Watching TV	

IDENTIFY YOUR TIME-WASTERS

Consider now in some detail the way you used your time last week. Write down four things which you found frustrating about the way you spent your time. The ideas below may help to fire your imagination. Circle any which are appropriate and add others of your own to the chart.

PERSONAL ORGANIZATION	losing things procrastinating being late rushing dealing with unimportant v. important
PERSONALITY FACTORS	worried tired lack of discipline butterfly mind lazy inflexible
HOME ISSUES	children's demands partner's needs housework relatives' requests financial matters
WORK ISSUES	too many meetings unreliable colleagues too much work too many interruptions unrealistic deadlines ineffective support
SOCIAL	too much travel too many committees pressure to conform pressure to do particular things too many 'phone calls/visits

Consider the questions which follow to give you further insights into your own feelings and attitudes concerning use of time in the week under review.

HAVE I WASTED TIME? **(ESTIMATE THE NUMBER OF HOURS)**	Personal Life: Professional Life:
HAVE I BEEN ORGANIZED EACH DAY IN **KNOWING WHAT I WANTED TO ACHIEVE?**	Personal Life: Professional Life:
HAVE I SPENT TIME ON ROUTINES THAT **WERE UNNECESSARY? (SPECIFY)**	Personal Life: Professional Life:
DID I PUT ANYTHING OFF UNTIL NEXT **WEEK?**	Personal Life: Professional Life:
HAVE I SPENT TIME ON ACTIVITIES THAT **COULD BE DONE BY SOMEONE ELSE?**	Personal Life: Professional Life:

HAVE I PRIORITIZED WELL?	Personal Life: Professional Life:
HAVE I MET DEADLINES?	Personal Life: Professional Life:
DO I ANSWER ALL MY TELEPHONE CALLS MYSELF?	Personal Life: Professional Life:
COULD I CUT DOWN ON TRAVELLING TIME?	Personal Life: Professional Life:
DO I NEED TO ATTEND ALL THE MEETINGS I GO TO?	Personal Life: Professional Life:

DO I USE ALL THE TIME SPENT TRAVELLING, WAITING FOR APPOINTMENTS CONSTRUCTIVELY?	Personal Life: Professional Life:
DO I SPEND MOST OF MY TIME REACTING TO OTHER PEOPLE'S DEMANDS?	Personal Life: Professional Life:
ON WHOM OR WHEN AM I SPENDING TOO LITTLE TIME?	Personal Life: Professional Life:
ON WHOM OR WHEN AM I SPENDING TOO MUCH TIME?	Personal Life: Professional Life:
HOW MUCH TIME HAVE I GIVEN TO WHAT I ENJOY? (ESTIMATE NUMBER OF HOURS)	Personal Life: Professional Life:

HAVE I FOUND TIME TO RELAX?	Personal Life: Professional Life:
HAVE I GIVEN MYSELF REWARDS FOR TASKS DONE?	Personal Life: Professional Life:

From my answers to the questionnaires and a scrutiny of the time logs what seems to be my major problem?

PERSONAL LIFE:
PROFESSIONAL LIFE:

You may have become aware as you were answering the questions, that many of the activities which give you real satisfaction in your personal and professional life are squeezed out by other activities. How do you balance what you would **like** to do against what you **must** do? The point in managing time effectively must be to increase the time you spend on activities which satisfy you.

List below the activities which give you satisfaction in your personal and professional life:

SATISFYING ACTIVITIES IN MY PERSONAL LIFE:

SATISFYING ACTIVITIES IN MY PROFESSIONAL LIFE:

HOW MUCH TIME WOULD YOU LIKE TO SPEND ON THESE SATISFYING ACTIVITIES?

Use the pie charts below to apportion the time **ideally**.
The more satisfying the activity, the larger the slice of the pie chart it will occupy.

Example

Satisfying activities in my personal life and the amount of time I would like to give to them as a proportion of my leisure time

Satisfying activities in my professional life and the amount of time I would like to give to them as a proportion of my work time

Now consider the actual time you spend on these activities.

Example

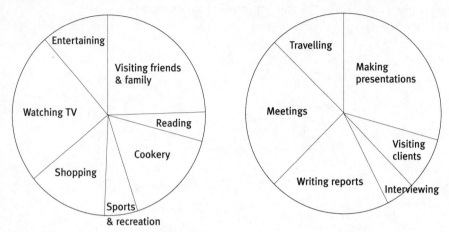

The above examples illustrate how some activities, e.g. watching TV, or making presentations, occupy far more time than is warranted by the satisfaction they offer.

Complete your pie graph below and note any similar discrepancies.

Actual time spent on satisfying activities in my personal life

Actual time spent on satisfying activities in my professional life

What surprises you about either of your pie charts? Have you thought of other activities which you have never got round to, which you would like to include in your plans for the future? E.g. taking up yoga, learning a language, updating computer skills, writing a novel.

List them below.

Activities I would like to pursue:

GUIDELINES FOR MANAGING TIME MORE EFFECTIVELY

In order to increase or decrease the amount of time you spend on some of your activities, you need to take a systematic approach. Think about the week ahead at home and at work. List all those activities on which you would like to spend more time. Keep in mind your committed time so that you don't become too ambitious.

Things I would like to do next week.

PERSONAL LIFE:	PROFESSIONAL LIFE:

Things I have to do next week.

PERSONAL LIFE:	PROFESSIONAL LIFE:

When you have Drawn up the Lists, Star Five Items in each Section Which seem to be Most Important to do

Try to put the items on your list in order of priority.

PRIORITIES FOR NEXT WEEK Personal Life (things I would like to do and have to do)	PRIORITIES FOR NEXT WEEK Professional Life (things I would like to do and have to do)
1.	1.
2.	2.
3.	3.
4.	4.
5.	5.
6.	6.
7.	7.
8.	8.
9.	9.
10.	10.

Copy out this list and put it somewhere where you can see it frequently during the week.

LIST MAKING

List making is an important tool for time management. The list is most usefully compiled as part of your daily routine, at the end of the day while you are still thinking about tasks you have to do for tomorrow.

THINGS I WOULD LIKE TO DO TOMORROW:

THINGS I HAVE TO DO TOMORROW:

By now you may be beginning to feel overwhelmed by your list of things to do. However, the list will appear far less daunting if you divide the tasks into three categories.

U   Urgent
I   Important
W   Can Wait

Put the items on your list into order of priority. List them in U, I and W importance and urgency. The urgent and less important tasks need to be done as quickly as possible in your day. As you go through the day complete the Us first, then the Is and finally the Ws. There is a great feeling of satisfaction in crossing off each activity from the list as you complete it. The crossing off acts as a reward. Even if there are only a couple of items crossed off you feel as if you have achieved something. At the end of the day transfer anything that is not completed to tomorrow's list. The relative urgency or importance can then be assessed in relation to that day's list of tasks.

You will find list making and prioritizing in this way a powerful tool for managing your time at home and at work.

Points to Remember:

- Always check that you have the list with you.
- Start the day with a short easily completed task to act as a motivator.
- Try to determine how much time each task will take as you code it.
- Build in extra time for certain jobs like shopping, interviews.
- Upgrade jobs that have been on the list for a while or cross them off.
- Don't put off irksome tasks – they will be staring you in the face tomorrow.
- Make sure you include tasks which you want to do as well as those you need to do.
- Add to your list whenever a new task occurs and code it appropriately.

It is best to transfer your list to a planner or diary. The ordinary desk diary can become one of your more useful management tools. Your diary can be modified to suit your needs.

It is useful to record everything including personal and social events in the diary since it is almost impossible to separate the various parts of your life from one another. Get into a regular routine of transferring your list to your diary each morning. It is possible to put some activities into the diary plan with a degree of certainty, e.g. planned meetings, interviews, lunch break. (Always set aside a time for lunch each day and try to go for a short walk to get away from the working environment.)

You may prefer to use a personal planner or organizer which would give you extra space for longer term plans, diagrams and charts in place of, or as well as, a smaller diary for essential daily information. The most important thing is to use something which suits you.

USING A DIARY AS A TIME MANAGEMENT AID

	FRIDAY		
8.00		TASKS	PRIORITY
9.00	Mail	look through applications for PA job	U
10.00	Prepare presentation	photocopy DHP	U
11.00	Phone William	phone Anne	I
12.00	Final planning meeting – Jill	write to John	W
13.00 } 14.00 }	Lunch		
15.00	Messages/telephone calls	REMEMBER	
16.00 } 17.00 }	Appraisal interview	organize car for Friday	U
17.00		Kate's present	W
18.00		Buy felt tips	W
19.00 20.00	Paul and Anne for dinner		

Try to follow these ideas for a week and at the end of this week, review your progress and ask yourself the following questions.

> How did using my diary help me; how did it hinder me?
> Did I get more done this week? If so, why?
> How did my priority of tasks change my working day?

In spite of listing and prioritizing everyday tasks in this way, you may still find you have insufficient time to complete satisfactorily the tasks you have to do, and no time at all for things you want to do. Consider how far other factors such as personal style, personal organization, home, family and social demands are contributing to your management problems. Identify some of your problem areas and find ways to minimize their effect. Refer back to the exercise you completed on page 185.

I WASTE TIME LOOKING FOR PAPERS, BOOKS, SCISSORS, CHANGE, ETC.

Keep your desk clear. Make sure each drawer is tidy and everything has a place.

Sort out all drawers systematically at home and at work and give everything a place. This makes sorting easy for everyone. Children need to be taught to replace things.

Have an amount of money in loose change for bus fare, charity collections, dinner money. Keep a filing system which is as simple as possible. Make sure filing is done every day.

I SEEM TO HAVE MORE CLUTTER TO DEAL WITH THAN OTHER PEOPLE.

Handle a piece of paper only once, file it, deal with it or bin it. When you receive a piece of paper consider *do I need to file this* – if not put it straight in the bin. Use in and out trays to keep your mail all in one place. Put things away as soon as you have used them. Regularly sort out drawers so that you can keep a check on items and things to discard. Take old clothes regularly to charity shops. Don't wait until sorting becomes a huge task! Do you need four knife sharpeners, three ice buckets (two of which leak), five old phone books, dried up bottles of correcting fluid, all those plastic bags, odd socks, old committee papers?

I TAKE ON TOO MANY TASKS. I FIND IT HARD TO REFUSE REASONABLE REQUESTS.

Learn to say 'no'. Delegate work to others – not only will this free your time for other things but it frees you to plan and organize. Delegate to your partner, to your children. (Don't underestimate children's ability. They can easily cope from a young age with many household chores. However, make it fun and teach them carefully. Don't give up and do it yourself!) Delegate to family and friends, and work colleagues. Consider your underlying reasons for lack of delegating. Are you insecure? Maybe by giving staff and family greater responsibility they will do the task better/prove you're unnecessary.

Do you worry about losing control? You may equate control with power and power with success. Maybe you feel you are losing out when other people take responsibility. Perhaps you feel that they can't really do the task. Incorporate training into your planning and save time in the long run.

> **I FEEL OVERWHELMED BY ALL I HAVE TO DO AND END UP COMPLETING LITTLE.**

Check that your list is realistic. Write down everything you hope to achieve rather than everything that needs to be done. Make sure you do the 'urgent' jobs first and work steadily through the list. Only do things which **need** doing. Do you have to make cakes, read junk mail? Do jobs which need more energy at your peak times. Are you a morning or an evening person? When your mind is at the most creative, tackle the day's most difficult tasks. Keep your not so good time for tasks that aren't too demanding. Constantly ask yourself 'Am I making the best use of my time right now?'

Combine activities; for example organize a working lunch with colleagues. Dictate ideas onto a tape for letters, action plans, shopping, etc. while you are travelling; traffic jams become far less frustrating if you can use the time constructively.

> **I OFTEN FEEL TOO TIRED TO GET WORK DONE EFFICIENTLY OR USE TIME CREATIVELY IN THE EVENINGS OR AT WEEKENDS.**

Take regular breaks throughout the day making sure you have lunch. Consider paying for extra help, secretarial, cleaning, childminding. Make your rotas and swapping arrangements more systematic. Ask friends and family for help. Use relaxation techniques while sitting at your desk or at the kitchen table. Plan your leisure activities well ahead so that the evening out is organized, tickets bought in advance, meals booked well ahead. It is often the effort of deciding what to do which makes for tenseness. Plan a regular treat for yourself at the end of each month – a massage, facial or pedicure, a new book, tape or video. It is important to look after yourself in this way. Try to get away for a weekend every few months with family, partner, or friends. A change of scene is enormously beneficial for everyone. Relaxation for many women means doing something completely different from their work. Have you a sedentary job, a thinking job? Perhaps a physical activity, a creative hobby working with your hands would offer a change? Have you a job where you are always on the move? Perhaps an interest which allows you to sit back and be entertained, concerts, theatre, music, sport events, would be appropriate.

Set yourself the task of doing one **new** leisure activity each week for the next four weeks. Identify what type of activity you most enjoy.

- being with people
- being alone
- taking exercise
- being creative

- being competitive
- being entertained
- travelling
- studying new topics

Get ideas of what is available locally from friends, the local paper, library facilities.

PEOPLE INTERRUPT ME AT HOME AND AT WORK OR STAY CHATTING LONGER THAN I HAVE TIME FOR.

Make sure people know you don't want to be disturbed. Use notices which state when you are available rather than 'do not disturb'. Be assertive in saying to people *I don't want to be unsociable, but I have to complete this report by 12 o'clock*, or *I must get my work done now, could I see you at 4 p.m.?* Use answerphones more. Where possible use other people to take calls for a period in the day. Write short notes instead of using telephones to avoid getting drawn into long conversations.

Don't invite interruptions by offering cups of coffee, leaving doors open, smiling at people as they go past, or immediately inviting them in. Do not saunter past other people's rooms.

I'M ALWAYS RUSHING AND OFTEN LATE.

Be sure to calculate carefully how long each task will take, then add 25 per cent extra time to allow for hidden time consumers.

It may be that you are underestimating the time needed to prepare for the tasks listed, your travelling time, time spent waiting or socializing.

Set realistic deadlines for each part of the task, and write them in your diary. If appropriate announce deadlines to family, friends and colleagues. Their interest may prompt you into action. Use external deadlines to help, for example, offer to chair a meeting or present a paper. Don't allow yourself to start anything new until you have completed the original task. When you have successfully met your deadline and completed tasks for the day, reinforce your efforts by rewarding yourself with something you really enjoy.

> **I SEEM TO BE TOO MUCH OF A PERFECTIONIST EVEN WITH MUNDANE JOBS LIKE CLEANING.**

Learn to relax your standards.

Apply a cost-benefit analysis in order to set appropriate standards. Taking less time to complete a task does not mean it is done badly. Try out the idea that some things are worth doing **adequately.** Six short notes to friends may give far more pleasure than one five page, beautifully composed letter which is long overdue.

If perfectionism is stopping you from doing things, or keeping you too long on one task, you need to ask yourself what drives your need to be perfect.

Unfortunately, you may be wasting your most creative hours doing routine tasks too well.

> **I SEEM TO WASTE HOURS ARRANGING OR WAITING FOR APPOINTMENTS.**

Use waiting time constructively. You could use it to relax, read, plan ideas or organize activities. Always carry a pen and paper, a book or small dictaphone if appropriate. Have toys, books or other entertainment to hand for children. Think positively about the extra time available. You may want to consider travelling to work at off-peak times if this is acceptable to your employers.

> **I SPEND TOO MUCH TIME SHOPPING.**

Shop weekly or monthly. Buy in bulk, food, stamps, envelopes, pens, tights – anything which you or your family run out of frequently.

In a prominent place keep a master shopping list which can be ticked (by everyone) as you run out of things.

Draw up a weekly menu so that you plan meals in advance before you shop. Shopping with your menu in mind means you are less likely to make impulse buys which are frequently wasted. Cook in bulk and freeze meals for two, three or four as required. Plan menus appropriately, for example, casserole Wednesday – everyone eating at different times – freeze one portion for baby-sitter's meal on Saturday.

MANAGING YOUR CAREER

Your career has the potential to be an important source of happiness, satisfaction and stimulation as well as offering security and financial reward. Your career development, therefore, deserves all the analysis, preparation and planning time you can afford. You need to be clear about what you want and need, what resources you have or need to develop, and how you are going to put your plans into action.

Identify first your personal needs and wants in your working life. These may be concerned with the type of work you would enjoy, the level of commitment which would suit you, the challenge demanded, the level of the security you need, or the work environment and so on. It is important to recognize that good working conditions, high salary and pleasant colleagues do not automatically guarantee satisfaction in your job. To be really satisfied you need to be sufficiently motivated. Motivator elements for you may be, for example, determining your work content or using creative talents. For others using communicative skills, feeling challenged or stretched may be the crucial factor. Think carefully and work out for yourself your own motivator factors. Write down as long a list as you can. Use the ideas listed to stimulate your own thoughts. Mark each box 1, 2, 3 or 4 to denote the category of importance, 1 being very important; 2 important; 3 slightly important; 4 unimportant.

Needs and Wants in my Working Life

high salary ☐

security ☐

opportunity to travel ☐

status ☐

variety ☐

feeling worthwhile ☐

independence ☐

interest ☐

organizing my own work content ☐

helping society ☐

supervision of my work ☐

pressure of work ☐

routine work ☐

working with others ☐

physically challenging ☐

Identify your strongest motivators by asking yourself: which of these makes me feel completely fulfilled and involved in my work.

My Strongest Motivators are:

Your next career management task is focused on assessing what you can do well, your ability or skills. Many people find difficulty in identifying the skills they use informally and every day. They take these skills for granted thinking 'everyone can do this'. Identifying the broad range of skills you can do well, however, is vital. Until you know what you are capable of you cannot make valid choices, market yourself or negotiate to achieve what you want. Neither can you make decisions about the best courses for you to follow to achieve success.

The next pages have lists of skills for which you are asked to rate yourself. This will be your subjective rating so it would be useful to ask a friend or colleague to rate you too. Think beyond your work-content skills and identify, too, those life skills which are more concerned with your personality and natural aptitudes.

Rate yourself 0–4	4	extremely good at this
	3	good
	2	fair
	1	not so good
	0	hopeless

Add your own ideas to the end of each list.

SKILLS WITH PEOPLE (INDIVIDUALLY OR IN GROUPS)

	Score 0–4
influencing, motivating, selling	
healing, curing	
assessing	
advising, counselling	
teaching, training	
communicating well in writing, orally	
negotiating	
making presentations	
leading	

SKILLS WITH IDEAS

	Score 0–4
creative writing	
composing through art and music	
designing new ideas	
collecting information by studying, researching	
being intuitive	
adapting, translating, developing projects	
acting	
working creatively with colour	
dealing creatively with shapes, spaces	

SKILLS WITH THINGS

	Score 0–4
fashioning, sculpting	
sewing, weaving, craftwork	
manufacturing, cooking	
maintaining, repairing	
painting and decorating	
assembling equipment	
precision working with tools	
being agile	
good physical coordination	
dexterity	
good hand-eye coordination	

SKILLS WITH INFORMATION

	Score 0–4
filing, classifying information	
managing money, budgeting	
following diagrams, or instructions	
computing skills	
analyzing, prioritizing information	
interpreting data, problem-solving	
proof-reading	
ability to manipulate numbers rapidly	
keeping track of data	

What does this Skills Audit tell you?

- For which category have you achieved the highest score?
- Does one ability area dominate your score or are your abilities spread across all four areas?
- Does your rating differ from your colleagues or friend?
- Do they see you differently?

Transferring your skills

You may have recognized that you have skills which go beyond the skill content of your present or past job. If you are a natural organizer, sales person, writer, counsellor, analyzer, manager or illustrator, then this skill is not restricted in its usefulness to one job or one activity; it is clearly transferable to many. Assessing skills under broad headings such as 'communicating well with groups and individuals' or 'working well to deadlines' gives you more flexibility to transfer them to another form of work. Don't undervalue your skills. First identify your abilities and then help potential new employers or your current employer recognize just how transferable some of your skills are.

Choose one activity which is one aspect of your work or current role. Write alongside the activity the transferable skills it gives you.

An Activity in a Current or Recent Work Role

EXAMPLE	TRANSFERABLE SKILLS
ordering equipment	organizing resources
	working to deadlines
	getting on with people
	understanding instructions
	making decisions

YOUR ACTIVITY	TRANSFERABLE SKILLS

Identify six transferable skills which you would like to use a great deal in your future career.

1.

2.

3.

4.

5.

6.

A closer awareness of the transferable skills used in your current or previous occupations or roles might stimulate you to think of ways to develop your career without necessarily having to retrain.

Your Qualities and Strengths

List your strengths – your positive qualities – including those which friends or colleagues would identify. Be as specific as possible and make the list as long as you can.

Your Achievements

What achievements in your life are you really proud of? Try to include different areas of your life, work and family, past and present, sports and hobbies. Write at least eight achievements.

Your Qualifications

Write down the qualifications you possess under relevant headings.

School Qualifications
   e.g. GCSEs, GCEs, etc.

College and university qualifications
   e.g. secretarial diplomas, degrees

Other courses attended

Professional qualifications

Qualifications may be an important asset in your career development but they are not a prerequisite for success. Many women have got to the top with no formal qualifications at all. However, you may decide that you want to acquire more qualifications now. Think about the type of qualification you need – vocational, academic or professional, the numerous ways in which you may gain them – part-time, distance learning, or weekend courses make for real flexibility. You may be able to secure help from your own organization or sponsorship to support the gaining of qualifications. Ask around for information. When choosing courses consider the qualifications you want to achieve for your own satisfaction as well as those you need for your career.

What qualification do I need/want for my career development?
What qualification would I like to get for my own satisfaction? (these may be the same)

TAKING ACTION – SETTING GOALS

Understanding your wants and needs, and identifying some of the things you've got going for you is an essential first stage in your career development. Sadly, this is as far as many people get because their wishes and objectives remain too daunting, too obscure or too ambitious. The clarification of goals and identification of steps to achieve them is likely to be one of the most important tasks of your career management.

The more attention you give to determining priorities and learning the decision making process, the more likely you are to recognize chances when they occur and have the confidence to take them. Remember the saying 'luck is the crossroads where preparation and opportunity meet'.

Consider these questions before you decide on your priorities for your career development:

* Does your previous or current job provide you with the values you consider important?

* Does it use your skills, strengths and qualifications?

* Are you able to change your job?

* Can you challenge your assumptions about your constraints?

* What do you need to discuss with others before you set your goals?

Choose one goal which you want to work on.

Example: to have a job with more responsibility
             to set up my own business
             to work with people
             to investigate changing jobs

Your Goal

You may have stated your goal clearly and realistically. However, check with the information below that this is so. A goal states simply **what** you want to achieve. It does not state when or how you will do so.

You need to make each goal:

CLEAR
Start with 'to', followed by an action word.

'To make an appointment . . . '

'To exercise on . . . '

SPECIFIC
Most goals are far too general.

E.g. 'to find a rewarding job', is not specific enough.

A specific goal would be:

'To find a job training people.'

MEASURABLE
Make sure you will be able to say whether or not you have achieved the goal. If the goal is stated in concrete terms, e.g. 'to get an interview for the manager's personal assistant' then this is measurable.

SET IN A REASONABLE TIME FRAME
State the time by which you want to achieve the goal.

E.g. 'to get promotion by January rather than, 'to get promoted later on in my career'.

MANAGEABLE AND REALISTIC
Make sure you have the necessary resources available to achieve your goal.

E.g. time, support

My work goal is:

To ...

I hope to achieve this by ...

Setting goals is important because they:

- help you to define what you want.
- give you a sense of direction.
- help you to get started.
- give you the impetus to make changes.
- give you a chance to concentrate time and energy on something specific.

What advantages are there for you in setting goals?

It is important to realize that your goals are constantly changing. You may need to take time every few months to have a fresh look at your goals in terms of importance and priority, and to set new goals.

FORCE-FIELD ANALYSIS

In any situation where you wish to make a change there will be some forces working against the change – things which weaken your resolve, and other forces which work towards the change and help you achieve your objective.

You will improve your chances of achieving your goal if you can identify and work on these helping and hindering forces **before** you move into action.

Example

The following diagram represents the forces working for and against Jill's goal which is:

. . . *to apply for promotion to personal assistant for the marketing director.*

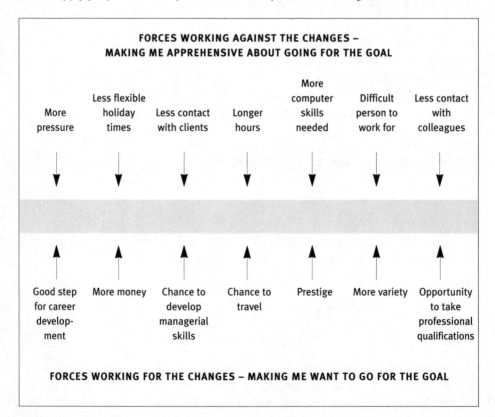

**FORCES WORKING AGAINST THE CHANGES –
MAKING ME APPREHENSIVE ABOUT GOING FOR THE GOAL**

| More pressure | Less flexible holiday times | Less contact with clients | Longer hours | More computer skills needed | Difficult person to work for | Less contact with colleagues |

| Good step for career development | More money | Chance to develop managerial skills | Chance to travel | Prestige | More variety | Opportunity to take professional qualifications |

FORCES WORKING FOR THE CHANGES – MAKING ME WANT TO GO FOR THE GOAL

On the chart provided below:

1. Write the goal you have chosen in the centre of the chart below.
2. List all the forces working in **favour** of what you want to achieve. Be specific (who, what, when, how much). *Circle the most important ones in green.*
3. List all the forces working **against** what you want to achieve. Be specific. *Circle the most important ones in red.*

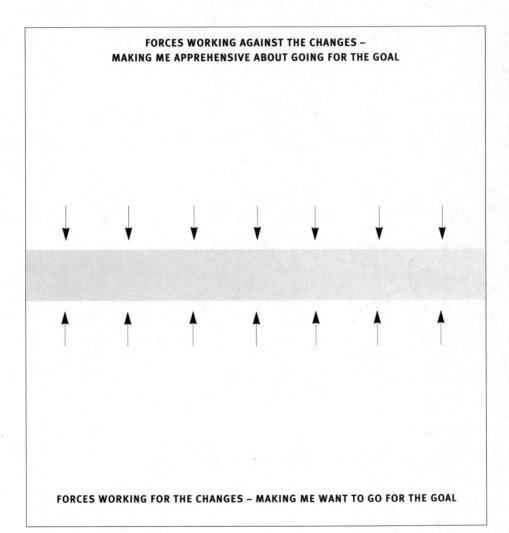

**FORCES WORKING AGAINST THE CHANGES –
MAKING ME APPREHENSIVE ABOUT GOING FOR THE GOAL**

FORCES WORKING FOR THE CHANGES – MAKING ME WANT TO GO FOR THE GOAL

Work on Each Force in Turn. Start with the Circled Ones, Finding Ways to Strengthen the Positive.

Example

One of Jill's forces pushing her towards her goal was:

. . . *opportunity to take professional qualifications.*

She could increase the strength of this positive by finding out which courses would be available and obtaining an outline of the course syllabus.

One strong force pushing me towards my goal:

I could increase the positive effect of this by:

Find Ways to Weaken the Effect of the Negatives.

Example

One of Jill's forces weakening her resolve was her concern that she would have less contact with current working colleagues. She could decrease the effect of this by organizing lunch or coffee breaks with colleagues or arranging to meet socially in the evenings.

One strong force weakening my resolve:

I could decrease the negative effect of this by:

DEVELOPING AN ACTION PLAN

You have now achieved what for most people is the most difficult part of managing career development – setting goals and identifying forces which may work for or against you.

Having clearly defined what you are going to do, the next step is to find a way to make it happen. You need to develop an ACTION PLAN. If the plan is to achieve action then it must be well structured.

Using the Step-by-Step Guide Below, Fill in your Action Plan on the Next Page.

1. State your clearly defined goal.

2. Break the goal down into all the small individual actions you will have to take to achieve the goal. Be as specific as possible. Writing them down will help you to see that one action, for example, *I must talk to my boss about promotion*, will involve you in planning a prior one, for example, phoning for a specific time for an interview.

3. Decide on one small thing you will do over the next week to make a start. Nothing is too small.

4. Arrange the steps into a logical order.

5. Put a date into your action plan when you are going to review your progress towards your goal.

6. Give yourself a realistic deadline.

- When you have completed your action plan, transfer the dates to your diary to remind yourself of the step deadlines.

- Involve others, family, friends, work colleagues to help you to stick to your action plan.

- If circumstances change or things don't work out as originally planned, don't abandon the action plan, just re-work your schedules.

Action Plan

MY GOAL IS . . .

Action steps I need to take (write them in any order).

Action Steps in Sequence

Step 1 to . . .

I will start this on .... (date)

Step 2 to . . .

I will start this on .... (date)

Step 3 to . . .

I will start this on .... (date)

Step 4 to . . .

I will start this on .... (date)

I will review my progress on .... (date)

I should know whether I have achieved my goal by .... (date)

PROGRAMME REVIEW

You have now reached the end of this self-development workbook in which you have looked at various aspects of your life from a new perspective. You have learned and practised a number of strategies and techniques to help you determine what you want to do and how to achieve the changes you have now decided you need. Run down the list of topics covered in the programme. Think about the significance of each of the topics in developing your potential in your personal and professional life; tick the appropriate column to determine where you will need to take action.

	I AM HAPPY WITH THIS	I NEED TO WORK ON THIS
BUILDING SELF-ESTEEM		
Understanding the importance of self-esteem		
How my self-esteem affects my life		
Challenging negative beliefs about myself		
Knowing what my positive qualities and strengths are		
Enhancing my self-esteem at home		
Enhancing my self-esteem at work		
Setting goals to maintain my self-esteem		
DEALING WITH STRESS		
Recognizing areas of stress in my life		
How stress affects me emotionally and physically		
Understanding how to take positive action to deal with stress		
Designing a programme of physical exercise to reduce stress		

Giving myself time to pursue hobbies, interests, relaxation techniques, etc.		
Feeling confident to cope with stressful situations		
Stress-proofing myself for the future		
DEVELOPING ASSERTIVENESS		
Being assertive with my partner		
Being assertive with my family and friends		
Being assertive with work colleagues		
Asking for what I want		
Refusing requests		
Giving praise and compliments assertively		
Handling criticism and aggression from others		
DEVELOPING MANAGEMENT SKILLS		
Managing my time in my professional life		
Managing my time in my personal life		
Managing my career		
Setting realistic goals		
Developing action plans		

Now you have identified several areas in your life where you need to take action. Recognition, however, is not enough. You have to want to change and dare to take action. Every day you can decide whether or not to take the risk – to take another step in your own journey to self-development. If one day you lose your energy and nerve and dare not take the risk, don't give up. You can renew your efforts the next day and have another go. You have the choice. You cannot rely on others to make it happen for you. Your partner, family and friends may support you, or not, but it's up to you to choose the life you want and take action to achieve it. *She who dares – wins*.

You may be feeling enthusiastic and inspired to put everything into practice at once! Do remember to start small and choose realistic goals. You may feel you need to refresh your memory from time to time; just revisit some of the chapters you found most useful.

We hope that you have enjoyed working through this self-development programme and that you have real success in fulfilling your personal and professional life.